RUSSIAN REGIONAL RECIPES

CLASSIC DISHES FROM MOSCOW AND ST. PETERSBURG; THE RUSSIAN FEDERATION AND MOLDOVA; THE BALTIC STATES; GEORGIA, ARMENIA AND AZERBAIJAN; AND CENTRAL ASIA AND KAZAKHSTAN

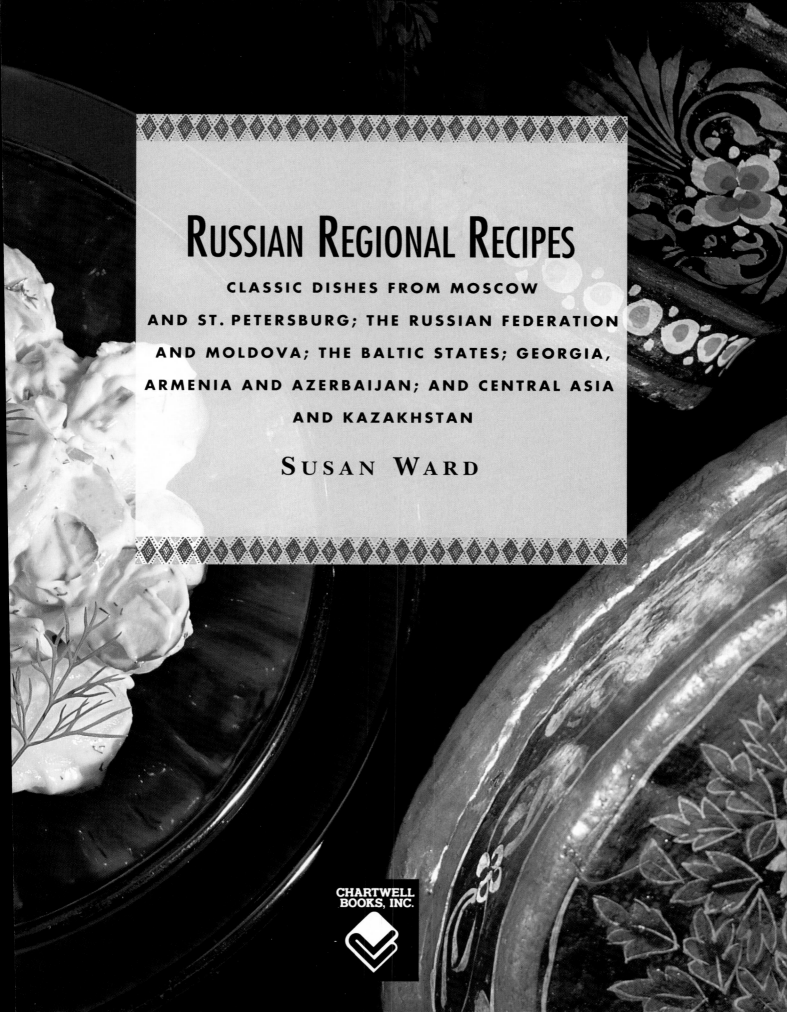

RUSSIAN REGIONAL RECIPES

**CLASSIC DISHES FROM MOSCOW
AND ST. PETERSBURG; THE RUSSIAN FEDERATION
AND MOLDOVA; THE BALTIC STATES; GEORGIA,
ARMENIA AND AZERBAIJAN; AND CENTRAL ASIA
AND KAZAKHSTAN**

SUSAN WARD

CHARTWELL
BOOKS, INC.

A QUINTET BOOK

Published by Chartwell Books
A Division of Book Sales, Inc.
110 Enterprise Avenue
Secaucus, New Jersey 07094

This edition produced for sale
in the U.S.A., its territories
and dependencies only.

ISBN 1-55521-905-5

This book was produced by
Quintet Publishing Limited
6 Blundell Street
London N7 9BH

Creative Director: Richard Dewing
Project Editor and Picture Researcher: Damian
Thompson/Katie Preston
Editor:Diana Vowles
Illustrator: Nick Day
Photographer:Trevor Wood

Manufactured in Singapore by
Eray Scan Pte. Ltd.
Printed in Hong Kong by Leefung-Asco
Printers Limited

Contents

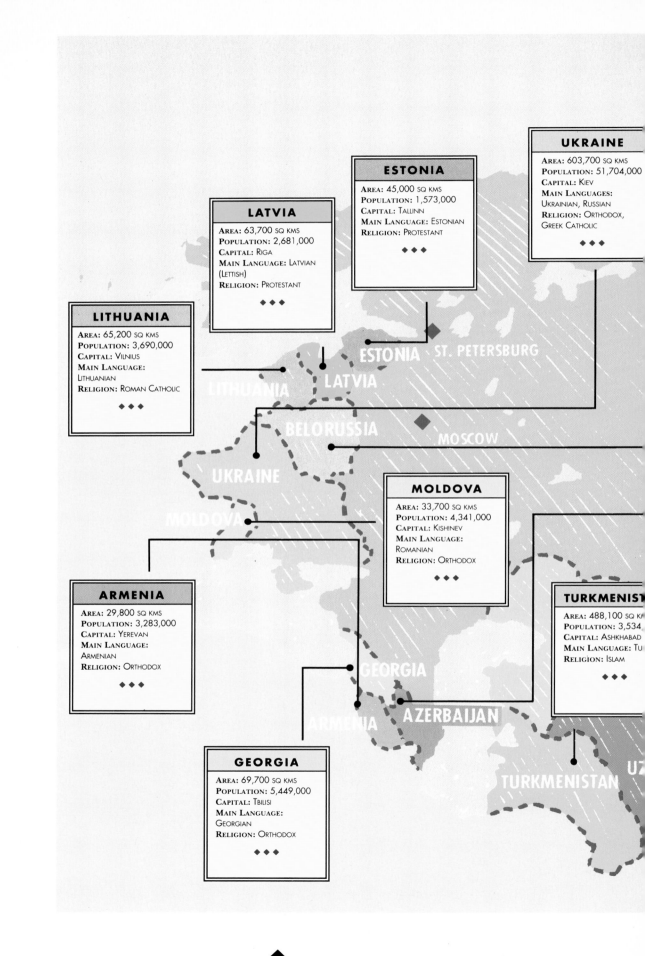

LATVIA

AREA: 63,700 SQ KMS
POPULATION: 2,681,000
CAPITAL: RIGA
MAIN LANGUAGE: LATVIAN
(LETTISH)
RELIGION: PROTESTANT

◆ ◆ ◆

ESTONIA

AREA: 45,000 SQ KMS
POPULATION: 1,573,000
CAPITAL: TALLINN
MAIN LANGUAGE: ESTONIAN
RELIGION: PROTESTANT

◆ ◆ ◆

UKRAINE

AREA: 603,700 SQ KMS
POPULATION: 51,704,000
CAPITAL: KIEV
MAIN LANGUAGES:
UKRAINIAN, RUSSIAN
RELIGION: ORTHODOX,
GREEK CATHOLIC

◆ ◆ ◆

LITHUANIA

AREA: 65,200 SQ KMS
POPULATION: 3,690,000
CAPITAL: VILNIUS
MAIN LANGUAGE:
LITHUANIAN
RELIGION: ROMAN CATHOLIC

◆ ◆ ◆

MOLDOVA

AREA: 33,700 SQ KMS
POPULATION: 4,341,000
CAPITAL: KISHINEV
MAIN LANGUAGE:
ROMANIAN
RELIGION: ORTHODOX

◆ ◆ ◆

ARMENIA

AREA: 29,800 SQ KMS
POPULATION: 3,283,000
CAPITAL: YEREVAN
MAIN LANGUAGE:
ARMENIAN
RELIGION: ORTHODOX

◆ ◆ ◆

TURKMENIST...

AREA: 488,100 SQ K...
POPULATION: 3,534...
CAPITAL: ASHKHABAD
MAIN LANGUAGE: TU...
RELIGION: ISLAM

◆ ◆ ◆

GEORGIA

AREA: 69,700 SQ KMS
POPULATION: 5,449,000
CAPITAL: TBILISI
MAIN LANGUAGE:
GEORGIAN
RELIGION: ORTHODOX

◆ ◆ ◆

ESTONIA ST. PETERSBURG

LITHUANIA LATVIA

BELORUSSIA MOSCOW

UKRAINE

MOLDOVA

GEORGIA

ARMENIA AZERBAIJAN

TURKMENISTAN U...

BELORUSSIA

AREA: 207,600 KMS
POPULATION: 10,200,000
CAPITAL: MINSK
MAIN LANGUAGE:
BELORUSSIAN
RELIGION: ORTHODOX,
ROMAN CATHOLIC

◆ ◆ ◆

AZERBAIJAN

AREA: 86,600 SQ KMS
POPULATION: 7,029,000
CAPITAL: BAKU
MAIN LANGUAGE: AZERI
RELIGION: ISLAM

◆ ◆ ◆

KAZAKHSTAN

AREA: 2,717,300 SQ KMS
POPULATION: 16,538,000
CAPITAL: ALMA-ATA
MAIN LANGUAGES:
KAZAKH, RUSSIAN
RELIGION: ISLAM

◆ ◆ ◆

THE RUSSIAN FEDERATION

RUSSIAN FEDERATION

AREA: 17,075,400 SQ KMS
POPULATION: 147,386,000
CAPITAL: MOSCOW
MAIN LANGUAGE: RUSSIAN
RELIGION: ORTHODOX, ISLAM

◆ ◆ ◆

UZBEKISTAN

AREA: 447,400 SQ KMS
POPULATION: 19,906,000
CAPITAL: TASHKENT
MAIN LANGUAGE: UZBEK
RELIGION: ISLAM

◆ ◆ ◆

ZAKHSTAN

KYRGYZSTAN

AREA: 198,500 SQ KMS
POPULATION: 4,291,000
CAPITAL: BISHKEK
MAIN LANGUAGE: KYRGYZ
RELIGION: ISLAM

◆ ◆ ◆

KYRGZSTAN

TAJIKISTAN

AREA: 143,100 SQ KMS
POPULATION: 5,112,000
CAPITAL: DUSHANBE
MAIN LANGUAGE: TAJIK
RELIGION: ISLAM

◆ ◆ ◆

INTRODUCTION

"DOBRO POZHALOVAT" – "WELCOME AND GOODWILL." THERE CAN BE NO BETTER INVITATION TO THESE PAGES THAN THE TRADITIONAL GREETING TO ANY VISITOR CROSSING THE THRESHOLD OF A RUSSIAN HOME. FOR THE RUSSIANS – INDEED ALL THE PEOPLES OF THE OLD RUSSIAN EMPIRE – ARE INTENSELY HOSPITABLE, A TRAIT FOSTERED BY BOTH GEOGRAPHY AND RELIGION. OUTSIDE THE CITIES, DISTANCES ARE GREAT, AND OFTEN MADE MORE DAUNTING BY INCLEMENT WEATHER, WHETHER THE ICE OF WINTER OR THE BEATING SUN OF SUMMER. IN SUCH PARTS OF THE WORLD TRAVELERS TEND TO BE GIVEN SUCCOR WITH A GENEROSITY UNKNOWN IN TAMER AND MORE POPULOUS REGIONS. AT THE SAME TIME, THE ORTHODOX CHURCH – WHICH HOLDS SWAY OVER THE MAJORITY OF THE OLD REPUBLICS – EMPHASIZES HOME AND CHRISTIAN FRIENDSHIP AS UNIFYING FACTORS IN THE COMMUNITY. THE MUSLIM CODE, AN IMPORTANT INFLUENCE IN SIX OF THE ASIAN REPUBLICS, PLACES SIMILAR IMPORTANCE ON HOME, HEARTH, AND HOSPITALITY.

Until the 20th century, traditional Russian hospitality was firmly anchored within the class system; there was no clarion call to break the bonds of social caste when entertaining. That had to wait until the ascent of Lenin – a man whose idea of a party was inevitably prefaced by the word "political."

Given these social strictures, however, both peasants and patricians extended not only the warm hand of friendship to their visitors, but as much food and drink as they could manage. The staples of the poorest peasant were bread and salt (*khleb i sol*); these were elevated to the position of customary twin offerings accompanying the words of welcome. Even today, they are presented to guests at public receptions, at private family gatherings, and at the traditional *Maslenitsa* celebrations to welcome the advent of spring. Thus the hospitality of the lowest spread to the highest.

Conversely, the tradition of serving *zakuski* (singular, *zakuska*) – a table of "small bites" – derived from the wealthy. It filtered down the social scale and throughout the Empire until it is now a fixture everywhere within the old Soviet sphere of influence, from the Baltic States to Caucasia and Central Asia.

The custom is thought to have originated on Chekhovian country estates outside Moscow, where long-distance visitors were greeted by an oval table groaning under a tantalizing array of pickles, vegetable salads, caviar, cured and creamed fish fillets, cold meats and pâtés, to be accompanied by warming shots of crystal-clear vodka. A substantial way of emphasizing the welcome initiated by the bread and salt, it was a kind of "happy hour" guaranteed to callers who dropped in any time from late afternoon to the dinner hour. In the early 20th century, hot dishes were added, and, later, *zakuski* became firmly anchored to

A highly polished samovar has center stage in the tea-time ritual of Mother Paisia, who has lived at the Phyti Russian Orthodox convent in Estonia for over 50 years.

NA ZDOROVYE – BOTTOMS UP!

Drinking in Russia and her neighbors is a serious business – whether it is alcoholically based or not! One of the most popular images in the Western mind is that of the great silver samovar dominating a table laden with Russian cakes and pastries. It is still a fixture of much Russian entertaining, though it is more often found in brass or stainless steel and is now electric, rather than heated by the charcoal-filled interior tube found in antique versions. On the top of the samovar sits a kettle with a strong brew of black tea. Hot water heated inside the samovar itself is drawn off by a spigot located at its lower front, and is used to dilute the dark, bitter tea in the kettle. The tea is then poured into tall glasses with metal holders, and garnished with thin slices of lemon. In parts of Caucasia and in Central Asia and Kazakhstan, green tea is preferred.

This technique of brewing, as well as the dried black leaves of the tea plant, was brought back to the Russian capital in the 17th century by the tsar's first explorer-ambassador to China and Mongolia, yet the heavily tannic beverage did not become well known until the reign of Catherine the Great in the 18th century. In the 19th century, the habit of tea-drinking spread from the landed gentry with their country tea parties to the urban bourgeoisie, and then to the masses.

Like tea, vodka ("little water") was initially the prerogative of the wealthy. Originally distilled from grape mashings, then rye, it was only in the mid-18th century that vodka began to be made from the imported potato. The folk mythology of the hard-drinking Russian was well-founded in fact; by that time the duties on salt and spirits were responsible for 30 percent of the government's total tax revenue. In the days of the tsars, drinking vodka could thus be regarded as a form of patriotism!

Today, the best vodka is made from wheat, and is distilled many times over. It should be drunk very chilled, in one gulp from a small glass, being preceded by a *zakuska* or at least a bite of black bread or a pickle to prepare the stomach. The ritual is then repeated again and again, until the appetite and the honor of the company is satisfied. The best unflavored vodkas are Pschenichnaya, Stolichnaya (slightly sweetened), and Moskovskaya (with a small fizz of sodium bicarbonate); flavored varieties include Zubrovka (a Polish bison-grass vodka), Pertsovka (a zippy pepper version), Okhotnichya (Hunter's vodka, with spices and herbs), and Limonnaya (a lemon-flavored variety).

While good American-style beer (*pivo*) is only usually available in hotels and hard currency shops (*beryoska*), mildly alcoholic near-beer (*kvas*) is sold on Russian streets during warm weather. The commercial version is fermented from a combination of wheat, rye, buckwheat, water, and sugar, and is sold in portable barrels wheeled around the city streets. They can be identified by the letters KBAC (*kvas*) stamped on the sides.

Most of the wines (*vino*) available in the CIS and Baltic States come from Georgia, Moldova, and the Crimea. Both robust reds and whites are produced in Georgia, though they can often be unpalatably sweet for Western tastes. Moldova produces light, fruity whites, while much of the CIS champagne comes from the Crimea. A surprisingly acceptable brandy (*konyak*) is a specialty of Armenia and, to a lesser extent, Azerbaijan.

---

dinner itself, a marriage between Western cocktails and canapes and a traditional first course.

Of course the lavishness of the spread was – and is – always dictated by the economic circumstances of the host, but the emphasis is on plenty. It is also on variety, and it was on the *zakuska* table that some of the earliest introductions from the southern republics made their appearance in the north: steak tartare (*Myaso po-Tatarsky*), lamb kebabs (*shashlyk*), spicy fruit compotes and pickled watermelon, stuffed vegetables such as peppers, eggplant and vine leaves, and vegetable caviars – the most common being made from eggplant (*baklazhannayia ikra*). The idea was soon adapted to local mushrooms and even to the ubiquitous beet.

In return, Russian-style *zakuski* are found today in the farthest reaches of the old Soviet Union – even if they sometimes seem oddly out of place. The widespread use of sour cream made from cow's milk (*smetana*) in the European states is replaced by *matsoni* in Georgia, *matsun* in Armenia, *katyk* in Azerbaijan, and *egurt* in Turkmenistan, all made with ewe's milk.

Ironically, the liberating transformation of the Union of Soviet Socialist Republics into the Commonwealth of Independent States – with the attendant non-participating states of Estonia, Latvia, Lithuania, and Georgia – has come at a time when culinary cross-fertilization has never been greater. While the members and non-members of the CIS eye one another suspiciously, attempting to assert as much local sovereignty as possible, restaurants like the Baku (Azerbaijani cooking), the U Pirosmani and Zaydi-Poprobuy (Georgian cooking), and the Ko-op Kafe Yakimanka (Uzbek cooking) are among the most popular in Moscow. It is somehow less surprising that decent Swedish, Italian, Indian, Arabian, and Tex-Mex restaurants, as well as the biggest McDonald's in the world, have all recently opened their doors in the capital. Ideology has demonstrably no place in the kitchen or at table in the new CIS.

Such gastronomic *glasnost* (openness) is to be welcomed, but warily. Most of the old state restaurants have always borne appalling reputations, and the competition of the newer cooperative operations will raise standards eventually, benefiting visitors and citizens alike, but the opportunity for exploitation is rife. There is a fascination with anything western, and an eagerness to attract foreign investment; corruption and scarcities bedevil the struggling supply infrastructure; and for over half a century the population has been starved of balanced historical perspective and creative inspiration. These combined factors are calculated to distort the present search for

Kvas (right) *is a traditional Russian drink made from pulled rye bread and honey, and fermented with yeast and sugar.* **Medok (left)** *combines* **kvas** *extract and honey, jam, and fruit juice, while the middle drink is a concoction of honey and cranberries, with wine added to improve the taste and aroma.*

cultural – here specifically culinary – pride. Salvation must lie with that fabled and inherent hospitality which will brave long lines, shortages and high prices, as well as resorting to bribery, to guarantee the best for guests. This desire to give pleasure, and to present the beloved Mother Country in the best possible light, is the most reliable indication that a return to pre-revolutionary food and traditions is a realizable ambition.

Russian Regional Recipes is both a celebration of things as they were and an anticipation of a renaissance already in its first stages. The collection of recipes on the following pages is composed of classics offered in ethnic Russian restaurants; of lesser-known regional dishes found in local homes and among immigrant communities abroad; and of interpretations of some historical recipes, making idiosyncratic ingredients and methods more acceptable to contemporary tastes.

The people of the Russian Federation and her neighboring states are famously sentimental. Emigrés in the West speak with longing of their lost countries, and are returning there in growing numbers, despite the personal cost.

Perhaps this cookbook can give some slight flavor of what they left behind – and what they hope to find in their reclaimed future.

Gastronom No. 1, St. Petersburg's most famous food hall, recalls the aristocratic opulence that could be found in Tsarist Russia.

THE RUSSIAN WAY OF EATING

BREAKFAST (*zavtrak*) is served late in hotels – usually between 8:00 and 10:00am. It can be even later in a private home – more like Western brunch, ending at 1:00pm. However, Western ways are ensuring that in urban centers, breakfast is becoming an earlier, rather than later, occasion.

In European "Russia," it usually consists of tea, accompanied by sweet buns, rolls, bread and butter, curd cheese (*tvorog*), and/or buckwheat porridge and buttermilk. In hotels in Moscow, St. Petersburg and other large cities, it may include other Western preferences such as fried or boiled eggs, cold cuts, fruit juice, and watery instant coffee, as well as more elaborate ethnic dishes such as curd cheese pancakes (*tvorozhniki*) or curd cheese fritters (*syrniki*). If breakfast were taken very early – for instance, on a farm – it might be followed by a second *zavtrak*.

LUNCH/DINNER (*obed*) has traditionally been the most important meal of the day, although that, too, is changing with the influence of Western culture and Western-style working conditions. A selection of *zakuski* – varying in elaborateness depending on whether it is a weekend or workday, a festive occasion or a family meal – may be followed by the option of soup, then a meat, fish or poultry course, ice cream, pudding or pastry, and coffee.

Lunch is a highly moveable feast, occurring any time from about 1:00 to 5:00pm. A weekend gathering or an important business lunch may linger for hours. If a second breakfast has been eaten, *obed* follows in the late afternoon.

TEA (*chai*) is a particularly unpredictable repast. During imperial times, the afternoon or evening tea ritual (*vecherny chai*) was a social imperative among the aristocracy and bourgeoisie, the later version a complement to the afternoon *zakuska* table. Cold cuts, cheese, cakes, pastries and biscuits, sweetmeats, and candied fruits would be accompanied by tea and cordials.

Today one is less likely to encounter afternoon tea, though it is occasionally served in Moscow and central Russia. Afternoon coffee and cakes in the Baltic region are more of an institution. Tea in the Levantine manner – taken lingeringly at any time in the afternoon at a teahouse (*chaikhana*) – is the custom in Azerbaijan, Central Asia, and Kazakhstan.

SUPPER (*ouzhin*) is yet another meal about which it is difficult to be precise. If two breakfasts and a late lunch were the order of the day, then supper would be very light or non-existent. Usually, however, supper can be any time from 7:00 to 10:00pm, and takes the form of a lighter *obed* with fewer *zakuski*, or perhaps just a soup, a main course, dessert, and no coffee.

On the other hand, late evening is often the time when city dwellers like to kick up their heels – in which case "supper" can go on until well after midnight, and consists mostly of a succession of *zakuski* accompanied by enormous quantities of vodka. The idea is not so much to have a meal as to have an uproarious time and become extraordinarily drunk!

In the village of Makhvilauri, in southwestern Georgia, a mother and daughter survey the harvest from their kitchen garden.

HERBS AND SPICES IN REGIONAL CUISINE

ALLSPICE (*pimient*)

The dried berries of the Jamaican pimento tree, combining the flavors of cinnamon, cloves and nutmeg, with perhaps a hint of pepper. Scandinavia is the world's major importer, followed closely by Russia and the western republics, which use large quantities in fish packing as well as in desserts, pastries, and spicy dishes.

BASIL (*bazilik*)

Both the purple and green varieties are used in Caucasian cooking, giving a depth of flavor to meat dishes, marinades, and salads.

CARAWAY (*t'meen*)

A relative of dill and fennel. The seeds are used to flavor pickles, fish, cabbage, sauerkraut, soup, pork dishes, and some pastries.

CARDAMOM (*cardamon*)

The pods and seeds are used in international cooking; the seeds only are included in Russian, Balkan, and Ukrainian pastries and pickles.

CINNAMON (*koritsa*)

True cinnamon is a native of Sri Lanka, the bark of the *Cinnamomum* tree, though the more bitter bark of Chinese species also goes by the name. It came to European Russia and the Baltic by way of the Levant and the southern empire, and is much used in pastries and desserts.

CORIANDER/CILANTRO (*koriandr*)

An herb which resembles flat-leaved parsley, and is sometimes used interchangeably with it in Georgian and Armenian recipes, though it has a more dominant, pungent taste. Sprigs can be frozen or preserved in salt and oil, but do not dry successfully.

DILL (*ukrop*)

A popular herb in most East European and Scandinavian cookery. The seeds and, especially, the feathery leaves, have a distinctive sweet-sour flavor much liked for pickles, fish dishes, and breads. Chopped dill leaves are also used as a garnish, for example for potatoes or sour cream.

GARLIC (*chesnock*)

Evidence suggests that this herb originated in Kirgizstan, and was brought to the northern Russian states by way of the Silk Road. It is much used in pickles and meat stews.

MARJORAM (*majoran*)

Used in Middle Eastern cooking, this herb has crept across the borders into spicy Caucasian dishes. A particular wild variety which does not grow outside the eastern Mediterranean region is much prized.

MINT (*myata*)

A herb ubiquitous in Caucasian and Central Asian cooking, added to tea, salads, many hot spicy dishes and fruit compotes, it marries particularly well with lamb and cucumber, both favored ingredients.

NUTMEG (*muscatny oreckh*)

A native of the Moluccas in the East Indies, this hard seed of the tree *Myristica fragrans* came north to Russia and Eastern Europe via the Silk Road and then the Baltic ports.

PAPRIKA (*krasny perets*)

A powder ground from the ripened seed pod of the red sweet pepper. The most prized – and sweetest – variety is that known as Hungarian paprika. It is used occasionally in Russian and Ukrainian cooking.

PARSLEY (*petruska kudryavaya*)

Only the flat-leaved variety is used. It has a slightly more marked flavor than the curly strain more commonly found in the West.

SAVORY (*chabyor*)

An atypical member of the mint family, having a sweetly piquant flavor much appreciated in the Georgian kitchen, where it is used in meat stews and marinades.

TARRAGON (*polyn estragon*)

A variety of European wormwood grown for its delicately pungent leaves. It is particularly evident in French and in Georgian cookery; in the latter it complements fish and lamb dishes, as well as vegetables and salads.

SUGGESTED MENUS

A REGIONAL MEDLEY DINNER
Mushroom caviar *(Gribnoy ikra)*
with sour-cream rye rolls
(balabusky)
•
Veal and liver pâté with pickles and radishes
(Pashtet iz tielyatiny)
(s ogurtsami i ryedisom)
•
Stuffed cabbage rolls
(Golubsty)
•
Sweet apple bread pudding with lemon sauce
(Sladky pudding z yaablokami i limonnoy podlivkoy)

A TRADITIONAL ZAKUSKA DRINKS PARTY
Flavored vodkas and/or vodka cocktails
•
Salmon and Cabbage-filled piroshki
(Piroshki z Iososemi Kapustoy)
•
Uzbekistan sweet walnut brittle
(Sladkoye pyechenye iz gryetskikh orekhov po-Uzteksky)
•
Marinated mushrooms
(Marinovannye Griby)
•
Steak Tartare
(Myaso po-Tatarsky)
•
Kazakhstan lamb potato cakes
(Kartophelnye piroshki z baraninoy po-Kazakhsky
•
Minsk-style eggs
(Jajka Minsky)
•
Deep-fried herb and Kale pastries
(Gutap)

A PICNIC EAST OF THE CAUCASUS
Yogurt soup with apricots and walnuts
(Sup iz yogurta z abricosami i gryetskimi orekhami)
•
Eggplant caviar with toasted pitta bread
(Baklazahannya Ikra)
•
Cold pheasant Georgian-style
(Phazan po-Gruzinsky)
•
Karabakh-style salad
(Salat po-Karabakhsky)
•
Dried-fruit and nut tart
(Tort iz sushyonykh fruktor orekhov)

~

A HEARTY WINTER LUNCH
Moldovan potato-cheese soup
(Moldavsky sup iz syra i Kartophelya)
•
Siberian meat dumplings
(Pelmeni)
•
Whipped eggs and sugar
(Gogol-Mogol)
•
Sweet caraway cookies
(Cepumi)

A COLD SUMMER LUNCH PARTY
Raspberry soup
(Malinovyi sup)
•
Lithuanian cottage cheese bacon bread
(Litorsky tworozhny khleb z beconom)
•
Chicken and potato salad
(Salat Olivier)
•
Transcaucasian cabbage and mint salad
(Transcavkazsky salat iz kapusty z myatoy)
•
Uzbekistan sweet walnut brittle
(Sladkoye pyechenye iz gryetskikh orekhov po-Uzbeksky)
•
Pickled watermelon rind
(Marinovannya arbuznaya korka)
•
Tea ice cream with rum sauce
(Chainoye morozhennoye z romovoy podlivkoy)

A REGIONAL FISH DINNER
Clear fish soup with dumplings
(Ukha z Katushkami)
•
Onion-and-mustard herrings
(Sipoli Mércé)
•
Sevan lake trout Yerevan-style
(Sevanskaya fovel po-Yerevansky)
•
Spinach and walnut purée
(Pkhala)
•
Oranges with spiced rum
(Apyelsing v romye z pryanostyami)

~

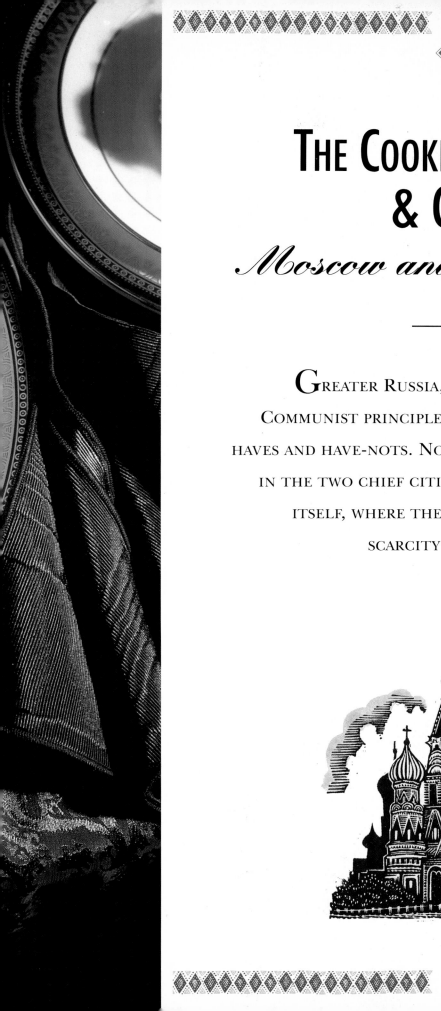

1

THE COOKING OF COURT & CAPITAL

Moscow and St. Petersburg

GREATER RUSSIA, EVEN IN THE HEYDAY OF
COMMUNIST PRINCIPLE, HAS ALWAYS BEEN A LAND OF
HAVES AND HAVE-NOTS. NOWHERE IS THIS MORE TRUE THAN
IN THE TWO CHIEF CITIES OF THE RUSSIAN REPUBLIC
ITSELF, WHERE THE WINTERS ARE HARSH AND
SCARCITY A FACT OF LIFE.

The opulent main staircase of the Hermitage Museum in St. Petersburg, one of the world's largest repositories of art, culture, and history.

In the days of empire, good eating was the prerogative of the aristocracy and the merchant classes; the peasants continued as they had for centuries at subsistence level. The triumph of the socialist state simply meant that that level was extended upwards, to give the greater number the opportunity to live, literally, on the breadline. The political elite, the *politburo* chiefs and state *apparatchiks*, continued to enjoy privileges denied the masses. Like the tsars and nobility of old, they had special suppliers and sources that were denied the common man. While the tsar had commanded his own fishing and hunting grounds, and was liberally gifted by foreign ambassadors with wines, cheeses and other delicacies, they had access to hard-currency supermarkets and the expensive state-run *Beryoskas*, selling imported luxuries like instant coffee, alcoholic drinks and sugar, as well as homegrown smoked sturgeon, caviar, and champagne (*shampanskoye*).

Even the geographical locales did not change. Moscow and Leningrad (now reverted to its pre-revolutionary name of St. Petersburg) continued as the dominant centers of the politics, learning, arts, and culture – in its widest sense – of the Russian Republic, and thus of the Union of Socialist States. Those few visitors who ventured behind the Iron Curtain almost inevitably went to these two historic capitals; but the uninspired, and often downright unpalatable, fare they sampled there had become a travesty of the great days of 19th- and early 20th-century *haute cuisine*.

That overused phrase is no misnomer in this case. Many dishes which later became internationally known were culinarily translated from the Russian colloquial by gifted French chefs. The great Anton Carême, who cooked for Alexander (*Alexi*) I, is probably the most famous, but many others followed in his wake, working not only for the royal family but also for the lesser nobility. Ethnic influences from the Russian heartland, from rich estates in the Ukraine and Belorussia, and from the lands of the south were refined by these culinary artists into recipes still exotic but now appealing to cultivated tastes. Dishes like *bef Stroganov, charlotte Russe (apple charlotte), steak Tartare,* and *rum baba* spread from Russian to Parisian society, and onto the *nouveau riche* tables of Delmonicos in New York.

A COSMOPOLITAN CUISINE

It is not only to the French, however, that the classics of the high table owe thanks. Earlier, trade with Byzantium and the exploitation and final annexation of Georgia, Armenia, and the Central Asian States had resulted in a range of wines, a tradition of sweet cakes and pastries, and an appreciation of fresh fruit and nuts. In the early 18th century, Peter the Great employed Dutch, German, and Swedish chefs. An initially bemused, then enthusiastic, court was introduced to sausages, hard cheese, fruit sauces, and compotes.

Perhaps it was the Swedes more than anyone, however, who influenced the style of entertaining, by tempting the hearty Russian appetite with an initial medley of tidbits – smoked fish, caviar, cold ham, preserved vegetables, and spicy pastries. An adaptation of their own beloved *smörgåsbord*, it was christened *zakuski* (small bites) in Russian. By the last years of the 19th century, it had evolved into an intricate marriage of the culinary and visual arts so lavish that foreigners understandably mistook it for the whole meal. The growing middle class in pre-Revolutionary Russia took the custom to their hearts and tables. Even in today's straitened circumstances, nowhere is the generosity and imagination of the native character made more apparent than in this traditional first act of a meal.

TRAVELER'S TALES

Today, the changes shaking up the Russian Republic present the visitor to Moscow and St. Petersburg with an uncomfortable paradox and a new variation on the theme of haves and have-nots. While tourists can eat well – and, more and more, exceptionally well – at the new cooperative restaurants, with a strict policy of hard currency only, which have sprung up all over both cities, on the streets the locals jostle to sell their services and possessions for food. If lucky, they will join the snaking lines of people at low-quality rouble cafés and shops, unless they have obtained dollars from a Western source.

It is difficult not to feel guilty at being able to buy a better lifestyle than the people who live there. At the same time, it is frustrating for the true traveler, who wants to experience a country without the divisive trappings that mark him or her as alien. Yet attempting to patronize restaurants where the Russians go can mean indifferent-to-awful food, long lines, and sometimes simply no success. A room of empty tables will be unaccountably declared full – and off you are sent to a hard currency establishment made for the likes of you.

It is to be hoped that the quality of the new restaurants will remain, while the restrictions on clientele and supply will eventually be eliminated. This, of course, would be the happy result of economic stability and reform for the entire country. At present, however, tourism is one of the few bright prospects for the historic capitals of Old Russia. Since the Iron Curtain has been torn asunder, the Western world has been looking – and venturing – in with as much curiosity as Russia's citizens have been looking out.

On Arbat Street, the towers of a Russian Orthodox cathedral and modern skyscrapers epitomize Moscow old and new.

Clear Fish Consommé with Dumplings

CLEAR FISH SOUP WITH DUMPLINGS

UKHA Z KATUSHKI

◆ ◆ ◆

Usually made with sturgeon in Russia, this light consommé can also be served with fish *pelmeni* (Siberian ravioli) instead of *katushki*, giving a Siberian twist.

SERVES 6–8

- ◆ 10 cups water
- ◆ 1 cup dry white wine
- ◆ 4 lb fish bones and trimmings (from white fish such as haddock, pike, whiting etc)
- ◆ 2 large onions, sliced
- ◆ 2 large carrots, thickly sliced

- ◆ 6 parsley sprigs
- ◆ 1 bay leaf
- ◆ 2 whole cloves
- ◆ 1 tsp black peppercorns
- ◆ 2 tbsp fresh lemon juice
- ◆ 1 tbsp finely chopped fresh dill

For the *katushki*

- ◆ 1¹/₂ lb white fish (haddock, pike, whiting fillets)
- ◆ ³/₄ in thick Greek, sourdough, or country-style white bread, crusts removed and soaked in a little water

- ◆ 1 egg
- ◆ ¹/₂ tsp fresh dill, finely chopped
- ◆ salt and freshly ground black pepper
- ◆ flour

To make a *fish stock*, place the water in a large saucepan and set over a high heat. Add the wine, fish trimmings, onions, carrots, parsley, bay leaf, cloves, and peppercorns. Bring to the boil, and simmer strongly until reduced by half – about 1 hour or a little more. Remove the carrots.

Pour the *fish stock* into a bowl. Rinse the saucepan and place a sieve over it. Line with damp cheesecloth and pour the *stock* into it. When the liquid has drained through, press the solids with a spoon to extract as much juice as possible, then twist the cheesecloth over the bowl to get the last drops. Discard the fish trimmings and vegetables. (The *stock* may be made in advance and chilled or frozen until needed.)

Now make the *katushki*. Remove any small bones from the fish and squeeze out the bread as much as possible. Process the bread and fish to a rough paste in a food processor or blender, then place in a bowl with the egg, seasoning to taste, and the dill. Knead with the hands until you have a firm mixture (if the mixture is not thick enough, add a little flour until it takes firm shape). Take out small handfuls of the mixture and form into olive shapes about ³/₄ in in diameter. Chill the dumplings for about 1 hour. (They may be kept in the refrigerator overnight.)

When ready to serve the soup, return the *fish stock* to a saucepan and bring to the boil. Reduce the heat to low, thinly slice the reserved carrots, and return to the saucepan. Gently drop in the *katushki*. Simmer the *katushki* in the broth until they are cooked, abut 10 minutes, then add the lemon juice. Spoon into individual bowls and garnish with dill.

SORREL SOUP WITH KIDNEYS AND PICKLES

RASSOLNIK

◆ ◆ ◆

A soup which crept from lowly origins to the highest tables in the land. This is a St. Petersburg favorite, served chilled as often as hot.

SERVES 8

- ◆ ¹/₃ cup butter
- ◆ ¹/₄ cup vegetable or sunflower oil
- ◆ 1 medium onion, finely chopped
- ◆ 1 celery stick, finely chopped
- ◆ 1 medium carrot, finely chopped
- ◆ 1 large potato, peeled and diced
- ◆ 1 lb lamb's kidneys, trimmed and cut into ¹/₂ in pieces
- ◆ ¹/₂ cup plain flour
- ◆ 6 parsley sprigs, chopped

- ◆ 2 lb fresh sorrel leaves or 1 lb each sorrel and young spinach leaves, stripped from their stems and finely chopped
- ◆ salt and freshly ground black pepper
- ◆ 6¹/₄ cups beef stock
- ◆ 1 bay leaf
- ◆ 2 sour kosher pickles, finely chopped
- ◆ ¹/₃ cup pickling juices
- ◆ 1 egg yolk
- ◆ sour cream

Melt ¹/₄ cup butter and most of the oil in a large saucepan, and gently sauté the onion, celery, and carrot until they are softened and lightly colored, about 10 minutes. Add the chopped potato and continue cooking, stirring for a further 5 minutes. Transfer the vegetables to a bowl and set aside.

Heat the remaining butter and oil in the pan. Dip the kidney pieces into the flour and gently fry them until they are slightly browned, about 3 minutes. Remove with a slotted spoon and set aside. Stir the parsley and sorrel (or sorrel and spinach) into the pan, and add the cooked vegetables. Toss everything gently until the leaves are wilted. Season to taste with salt and pepper, and add the beef stock and bay leaf. Bring to the boil, then cover, lower the heat, and simmer for about 25 minutes.

Remove the bay leaf and mash the vegetables to thicken the soup. Stir in the pickles and their juice, together with the cooked kidneys. Simmer for a further 5 minutes.

Remove a cupful of the soup and beat with the egg yolk in a small bowl. Stir the egg mixture back into the soup and heat it briefly. Do not boil or the egg will curdle.

If serving hot, transfer the soup to a large tureen and pass the sour cream separately. If serving cold, cool to room temperature, then chill for 2–3 hours before dividing between individual bowls, each topped with a spoonful of sour cream.

ASPARAGUS VEAL BROTH

BAGRATION

◆ ◆ ◆

This elegant consommé was named for Prince Bagration, the Georgian general felled by Napoleon's troops at the Battle of Borodino, outside Moscow, in 1812. Though the battle ended in a draw, it marked an important moment in Russian nationalism, culminating in the French emperor's ignominious retreat from the capital.

SERVES 6

◆ *¹/₄ cup sunflower oil*
◆ *3 lb veal trimmings and bones*
◆ *2 large onions, finely chopped*
◆ *2 large carrots, peeled and chopped*
◆ *2 x 14 oz cans of chicken consommé*
◆ *2 bay leaves*

◆ *¹/₂ tsp crumbled fresh thyme*
◆ *3 egg whites*
◆ *salt and freshly ground white pepper*
◆ *1 lb baby asparagus tips*
◆ *sour cream*
◆ *fresh dill sprigs*

Heat the oil in a large saucepan. Add the veal trimmings and bones, and toss them in the oil over medium heat until browned all over, about 15–20 minutes.

Add the chopped vegetables, and continue to cook until they are lightly colored and softened. Add the chicken consommé, bay leaves and thyme, adding water, if necessary, to cover the meat, bones, and vegetables. Bring to the boil, and continue to cook vigorously for 15 minutes, skimming off the scum that rises to the surface. Then reduce the heat, cover, and simmer for 2 hours.

Allow the stock to cool slightly then strain it into a bowl, pressing hard on the meat and vegetables to extract as much juice a possible. Cover, cool, and chill for at least 12 hours or overnight.

Pour half the stock into containers and freeze for future use. Of the remainder, pour 1¼ cup into a large bowl and the rest into a saucepan.

Beat the egg whites into the stock in the bowl. Bring the stock in the saucepan to the boil then, in a stream, pour into the egg-white stock, beating all the while. Pour the combined stock into the saucepan, and bring to a simmer over moderate heat, whisking constantly. When just simmering, reduce the heat to low, stop stirring, and let the stock simmer uncovered for 25 minutes.

Line a sieve with several layers of cheesecloth or absorbent paper towels and place over a clean saucepan. Slowly ladle the stock and congealed egg whites into the sieve, trying to disturb the whites as little as possible. The resultant consommé should be clear and delicate, leaving the impurities adhering to the whites in the sieve.

Place the strained stock over high heat. Season to taste with salt and white pepper, and bring to the boil. Add the asparagus tips, and cook for about 4 minutes. Divide the asparagus between the bowls, and ladle the consommé over it. Garnish each serving with a dollop of sour cream and a fresh dill sprig.

MUSHROOM CAVIAR

GRIBNOY IKRA

◆ ◆ ◆

Eastern Europeans, particularly Russians and Poles, are mushroom fanatics. Dawn expeditions into the wooded countryside in search of fungi are a common sight in autumn.

SERVES 8–10

- ◆ *12 oz fresh mushrooms (the more varieties, the better – field, shiitake, oyster, girolle, etc), finely chopped*
- ◆ *1 medium onion, finely chopped*
- ◆ *¹/₂ cup butter*
- ◆ *1 tbsp dry sherry*
- ◆ *¹/₃ cup curd cheese*
- ◆ *¹/₃ cup full-fat cream cheese*
- ◆ *3 tbsp fresh parsley finely chopped*
- ◆ *2 tbsp fresh tarragon finely chopped*
- ◆ *2 tbsp fresh marjoram, finely chopped*

In a large frying pan, sauté the mushrooms and onion in the butter over medium heat, stirring often. When the mushrooms are browned and softened, add the sherry. Remove from the heat.

In a bowl, beat together the two cheeses and herbs. Stir in the mushrooms, onion and their juices. Beat the mixture with a wooden spoon until it is well combined. Spoon the pâté into a small crock, smooth, swirl the top, and cover. Chill overnight or up to three days before serving with small rye rounds.

VEAL AND LIVER PATE

PASHTET IZ TIELYATINY

◆ ◆ ◆

Pashtet **can be made with veal and liver, pork and liver, or just liver; it can be served plain, set in aspic, or baked in pastry. This is a fairly simple recipe enlivened with dried mushrooms, a favorite Ukrainian ingredient.**

SERVES 8

- ◆ $\frac{1}{2}$ *lb calves' liver, chopped*
- ◆ *1 cup milk*
- ◆ $\frac{1}{4}$ *cup butter*
- ◆ $\frac{1}{2}$ *lb bacon, sliced*
- ◆ *1 small onion, chopped*
- ◆ *1 stick celery, chopped*
- ◆ *1 small carrot, chopped*
- ◆ *1 bay leaf*
- ◆ *4 peppercorns*
- ◆ $\frac{1}{2}$ *lb lean veal, chopped*

- ◆ *1 cup chicken consommé or stock*
- ◆ $\frac{1}{3}$ *cup dried boletus or porcini mushrooms*
- ◆ *2 slices stale white bread, crusts removed*
- ◆ *2 small eggs*
- ◆ *pinch of allspice*
- ◆ *salt and freshly ground black pepper*

In a bowl, soak the calves' liver in the milk for 1 hour. Drain thoroughly, and discard the milk.

In a frying pan with a lid, melt the butter over medium heat and coarsely chop and fry three-quarters of the bacon for 3–4 minutes. Add the onion, celery, carrot, bay leaf, peppercorns, and veal; toss to coat in the bacon fat and butter for a few minutes. Then pour in the chicken stock, and add the dried mushrooms. Cover and simmer gently for 1 hour. Add the liver and cook for a further 30 minutes.

Remove from the heat. Strain the stock into a bowl, and soak the bread in it for 5 minutes. Squeeze out as much moisture from the bread as possible, and process in batches with the meat and vegetables in a blender or a processor fitted with a metal blade. As the mixture is ground up, transfer to a large bowl. With the hands, work in the eggs, allspice, and salt and more pepper to taste.

Preheat the oven to 350°F. Line a 9x5x3 in loaf tin with the remaining bacon. Pack in the meat mixture, smooth the top, and cover the tin with foil. Bake for 45–60 minutes, until the pâté is browned and a wooden cocktail stick inserted in it comes away clean. Cool, remove from the tin, then chill. Serve in thick slices with black bread and butter and pickled gherkins.

Buckwheat Crêpes with Caviar

BUCKWHEAT CREPES WITH CAVIAR

BLINI Z IKRA

◆ ◆ ◆

Leaving the batter for the *blinis* **to stand overnight allows it to acquire its distinctive sour flavor.** *Blinis* **freeze well, and are delicious paired with smoked salmon or smoked meats such as ham and turkey, and with cottage cheese accompanied by dried or fresh soft fruits.**

SERVES 8–10

- ◆ ¹/₃ cup plus 1 tbsp lukewarm water
- ◆ 1 tbsp (¹/₄ oz packet) active dry yeast
- ◆ 2 tbsp sugar
- ◆ 2 cups milk
- ◆ 1 cup unsalted butter, melted
- ◆ 1 cup buckwheat flour
- ◆ 1 cup plain flour
- ◆ 1 tsp salt
- ◆ 2 large eggs, separated, at room temperature
- ◆ ³/₄ cup sour cream
- ◆ 1 cup black caviar or lumpfish roe
- ◆ 1 cup golden or red salmon roe

Pour the lukewarm water into a small bowl. Sprinkle the yeast and 1¹/₂ tsp sugar over it, and leave for 3 minutes. Stir to dissolve completely, then set in a warm spot for another 5 minutes, until it is foamy and doubled in volume.

Heat 1 cup milk to lukewarm, and stir into the yeast mixture together with the remaining sugar and 2 tbsp butter. Beat in the buckwheat flour for about 1¹/₂ minutes, then cover tightly with plastic wrap and chill it overnight.

Next day, let the batter come to room temperature. Heat 1 cup milk to lukewarm, and stir into the batter together with the plain flour, salt, egg yolks, and sour cream. Beat the mixture for about 1 minute, then cover and leave to rise for 1 hour or until foamy and doubled in size. In a metal bowl, beat the egg whites to stiff peaks. Fold them gently into the batter.

Place a griddle or a shallow frying pan over medium heat and, when it is hot, brush lightly with butter. Drop about 3 tbsp batter onto the griddle so that it spreads into a 3–4 in circle. Repeat twice, and fry the blinis for 2 minutes, or until the undersides are golden. Brush the tops lightly with melted butter, and turn them over to cook for 1 more minute. Repeat until all the batter is used up, meanwhile keeping the blinis warm, covered with foil, in the oven set at 250°F. (The blinis may be made up to 2 days before and kept covered and chilled. Reheat in a 350°F oven for 15 minutes.)

Serve the warm blinis wrapped in a napkin on a heated platter, accompanied by pots of the caviar and roe in ice and an attractive arrangement of sour cream, finely chopped hard-boiled eggs, sliced lemon, and snipped dill.

STUFFED EGGS, RUSSIAN-STYLE

YAITSA PO-RUSSKI

◆ ◆ ◆

While the origins of this dish lie within the borders of the Austro-Hungarian rather than the Russian Empire – it was a favorite of turn-of-the-century Viennese chefs – the marriage of ingredients justifies the name they gave it.

SERVES 6

◆ 6 hard-boiled eggs, halved
◆ 2 tbsp mayonnaise
◆ ¹/₂ tsp dry mustard powder
◆ 1 tbsp Dijon mustard
◆ 3 tbsp finely chopped sour-sweet pickles
◆ 2 tsp finely chopped scallions
◆ salt and freshly ground black pepper

To garnish
◆ capers ◆ paprika

Remove the yolks from the halved eggs, reserving the whites, and place them in a small bowl. Mash them thoroughly, then blend the mayonnaise, the two mustards, the chopped pickles, scallions, and seasoning to taste. Spoon the mixture into the egg-white halves, and garnish decoratively with the capers and paprika.

SALMON AND CABBAGE-FILLED PIROSHKI

PIROSHKI Z LOSOSEM I KAPUSTOY

◆ ◆ ◆

These *piroshki* are wrapped in yeast dough, a Ukrainian influence. Their contents and small size make them perfect for stylish drinks parties. Raise a glass of Abrau-Durso – Russian champagne – and down one of these little treats!

MAKES ABOUT 20

- ◆ *2–3 dried boletus or other wild mushrooms*
- ◆ *1 lb cabbage, cored and trimmed of old leaves*
- ◆ *3 tbsp unsalted butter*
- ◆ *salt and freshly ground black pepper*

- ◆ *$1/4$ lb salmon fillet*
- ◆ *2 tbsp sour cream*
- ◆ *1 tbsp caraway seeds*
- ◆ *1 tbsp dill seeds*
- ◆ *1 egg*

For the dough

- ◆ *$1/4$ cup lukewarm water*
- ◆ *1 tbsp sugar*
- ◆ *$2^1/2$ tsp ($1/4$ oz packet) active dry yeast*
- ◆ *$1^3/4$ cup plain flour*

- ◆ *$1^1/2$ tsp salt*
- ◆ *$3/4$ cup warm milk*
- ◆ *scant $1/2$ cup unsalted butter, melted*
- ◆ *2 large eggs*
- ◆ *oil*

Make the dough first. Place the water in a small bowl and sprinkle 1 tsp sugar and the yeast over it. Leave to stand for 15 minutes, or until foamy. In a larger bowl, combine three-quarters of the flour with the salt. Make a well in the center, and pour in the yeast mixture, the milk, the melted butter, the eggs, and the rest of the sugar. Using your hands, turn the dry ingredients into the wet, and combine thoroughly until you have a soft dough. Remove to a floured board and knead, adding more flour if necessary, to keep it pliable and not sticky. Continue kneading until the dough begins top blister.

Form the dough into a ball with your hands, and place it in an oiled bowl, turning to cover with oil. Cover with plastic wrap and let the dough rise in a warm place until it has doubled. Knock it down, cover, and chill overnight.

To make the filling, soak the mushrooms in hot water for 30 minutes. Drain, and chop them finely. Shred the cabbage in a food processor, then chop into shorter lengths. Place in a large saucepan of boiling water and boil for 3 minutes. Drain, refresh under cold water, and drain again, squeezing out the excess water.

In a large frying pan, sauté the cabbage in the butter for about 15 minutes. Season to taste and stir in the salmon and the mushrooms, tossing just enough to combine. Stir in the sour cream, then the caraway and dill seeds. Take off the heat, cool, then chill for 30 minutes.

Divide the ball of dough in half. Return one half to the fridge and roll out the other into a thin rectangle. Cut out $3^1/2$ in rounds with a cookie cutter or lid. Reserve the remaining scraps.

Preheat the oven to 400°F. Make an egg wash by beating the egg with a pinch of salt. Place a heaped teaspoon of the filling on each round, brush the edges with some of the wash, and fold over to make a crescent, pinching the edges together. Use the scraps to make further *piroshki*. Place them on a lightly greased baking sheet, cover with a towel, and allow to rise for 15–20 minutes. Brush the tops with the wash, and bake in the oven for 20–25 minutes or until they are lightly golden.

Roll out the remaining dough, and bake in a similar fashion. (The *piroshki* can be baked ahead and frozen. Defrost, and reheat at 350°F for 10–15 minutes.)

A distinguished feature of the Mikhailovsk Bridge in St. Petersburg are its cast-iron fences.

CHICKEN LIVERS IN MADEIRA SAUCE

PYECHYEN KUR V MADERE

◆ ◆ ◆

Served on its own, this recipe is a classic *zakuska*. but it is so delicious – and so rich – that it would make an elegant and inexpensive main course. Spoon it over rice or, more authentically, use to fill dinner-sized puff-pastry cases.

SERVES 4–6

- ◆ *1 1/2 lb chicken livers*
- ◆ *milk*
- ◆ *1/4 cup butter*
- ◆ *1 onion, sliced*
- ◆ *salt and freshly ground black pepper*
- ◆ *1 cup flour*
- ◆ *3/4 cup chicken stock*
- ◆ *1/2 cup Madeira*
- ◆ *scant 1/2 cup sour cream*
- ◆ *fresh parsley, finely chopped*

Immerse the chicken livers in milk to just cover, and soak for 2 hours. Drain thoroughly, and discard the milk.

Melt the butter over medium heat, and sauté the onion until softened. Dip the chicken livers in seasoned flour, and add to the onions. Fry gently until just colored, about 5 minutes. Stir in the stock and the Madeira, cover, and simmer for about 10 minutes, or until the livers are tender. Season the sauce to taste.

Transfer the livers to a bowl; boil the sauce until it is well reduced. Turn down the heat and whisk in the sour cream, a little at a time. Return the livers to the pan, spoon the sauce over, and heat through gently. Serve immediately, sprinkled with fresh parsley.

CHICKEN OR VEAL AND PORK CUTLETS

KOTLETY POJARSKI

◆ ◆ ◆

These patties are encountered all over Russia in varying degrees of digestibility – from execrable to excellent. The latter are frequently served with the sauce given below.

SERVES 6

- ◆ *1 1/2 lb finely chopped chicken or mixture of 3/4 lb each veal and pork, well-chilled*
- ◆ *2 1/3 cups fine fresh breadcrumbs*
- ◆ *1/3 cup unsalted butter, softened*
- ◆ *1/2 cup heavy cream*
- ◆ *large pinch of nutmeg*
- ◆ *salt and freshly ground black pepper*
- ◆ *2 large eggs, beaten*
- ◆ *2 tbsp vegetable oil*

For the sauce

- ◆ *1/4 cup unsalted butter*
- ◆ *1 small onion, chopped*
- ◆ *1 cup dry white wine*
- ◆ *1 cup chicken or beef stock*
- ◆ *2 tsp flour*
- ◆ *1 tbsp Dijon-style mustard*
- ◆ *2 tbsp fresh lemon juice or sour cream*

In a blender or a food processor, combine the chopped poultry or meats with 3/4 cup breadcrumbs, 1/4 cup butter, the cream, nutmeg, and salt and pepper to taste. Process until the mixture reaches the consistency of paste. Remove, form into 6 cutlet-shaped patties, and place on waxed paper. Chill for at least 2 hours.

Meanwhile, start the sauce. In a stainless steel or enamel saucepan, melt 4 tsp butter, and gently sauté the onion until it is softened. Stir in the white wine and the stock, and bring to the boil. Reduce the heat and simmer, uncovered, for about 10 minutes, then set aside.

Using your fingers, knead the flour into the remaining butter. Increase the heat of the stock and drop in the flour and butter mixture bit by bit, stirring all the time. When the sauce is thickened, remove from the heat.

Take the cutlets from the refrigerator. Place the beaten eggs in a shallow bowl and the remaining breadcrumbs on a plate. Dip each of the cutlets into the beaten egg, shaking off the excess, and then press into the breadcrumbs, coating each side well. Chill for another hour.

Heat the remaining butter and the oil in a large saucepan and fry the cutlets, 3 at a time, over medium-high heat for 4–5 minutes each side, or until golden-brown and cooked through. Remove and keep warm.

Finish the sauce by reheating it gently, stirring. Stir in the mustard and lemon juice or sour cream.

CHICKEN AND POTATO SALAD

SALAT OLIVIER

◆ ◆ ◆

A near relative of the "Russian salad" so dear to the hearts of caterers and delicatessen owners, this real Russian salad is a traditional favorite, again refined and Frenchified by an imported chef. It would make a delicious main course for a summer luncheon or picnic.

SERVES 6

- $1\frac{1}{2}$ lb cooked, boned, and skinned chicken
- 5 hard-boiled eggs
- $\frac{1}{2}$ lb baby or small red potatoes, boiled in their skins and thinly sliced
- 1 cup cooked fresh or frozen peas, drained
- $\frac{3}{4}$ cup mayonnaise
- $\frac{1}{2}$ cup sour cream
- 2 tsp Worcestershire sauce
- salt and freshly ground black pepper
- 1 tbsp chopped fresh dill
- black olives, halved
- 2 large sour pickles, finely chopped
- 2 tbsp capers

Slice the chicken into $\frac{1}{2}$ in wide strips. Finely chop two of the eggs. Place the chicken and chopped eggs in a large bowl, together with the potatoes, peas, and pickles. In a smaller bowl, beat together the mayonnaise and the sour cream. Fold the Worcestershire sauce and half the dressing into the chicken mixture, seasoning to taste.

To serve in the Russian manner, mound the chicken salad in the center of a large serving dish. Slice the remaining eggs, and arrange the slices around the salad. Top each slice with a halved olive. Spoon the remaining dressing over the salad, and scatter the chopped dill and capers over the top. Chill for 30 minutes before serving.

BEEF STROGANOFF

BEF STROGANOV

◆ ◆ ◆

The Stroganovs became one of the wealthiest members of the merchant aristocracy through their exploitation of Siberia's fur resources. The French chef of a late 19th-century Count Stroganov created this now internationally popular dish. It should *not* be served over rice – a heresy introduced by the West – but a tuft of straw potatoes on top is classically acceptable.

SERVES 6–8

- ◆ *1 tbsp dry mustard powder*
- ◆ *1 tbsp sugar*
- ◆ *6 tbsp sunflower oil*
- ◆ *3 large onions, sliced*
- ◆ *1 lb fresh button or field mushrooms, sliced*
- ◆ *2¹/₂ lb fresh beef fillet, cut into ¹/₂ in wide strips*
- ◆ *salt and freshly ground black pepper*
- ◆ *2¹/₂ cups sour cream*
- ◆ *6 fresh parsley sprigs, stems removed, chopped*
- ◆ *deep-fried straw potatoes (optional)*

Combine the mustard and sugar in a bowl with water to make a paste. Let the flavors mingle while completing the recipe.

Heat half the sunflower oil in a large, heavy-bottomed shallow casserole. When just crackling, add the sliced onions, reduce the heat to low, and stir. Gently soften the onions, covered, for about 25 minutes, stirring occasionally. During the last 10 minutes, uncover and add the mushrooms. Remove from the heat, drain the mixture, and set aside in a bowl.

Heat the remaining oil in the casserole. Drop in half the meat, stirring with a wooden spoon and turning the strips over to brown evenly. Transfer with a slotted spoon to the bowl with the vegetables; sauté the remaining meat. When all is browned, return the meat and vegetables to the casserole, together with the mustard mixture. Season to taste and add the sour cream, a little at a time, stirring continuously. Cover the casserole, heat through gently for about 5 minutes, and serve. Top each serving with a light scattering of parsley, and the straw potatoes, if desired.

SADDLE OF VENISON

OLENYA SEDLO

◆ ◆ ◆

**The aristocrat of game dishes, today venison is rarely
seen on even the most expensive restaurant menus in major
cities. Only in the wooded countryside, particularly
in the belt around St. Petersburg, can families enjoy this
prize of the hunter's bag.**

SERVES 6–8

- 5 lb saddle of young venison
- salt and freshly ground black pepper
- 8 slices bacon
- scant 2 cups beef stock
- ³/₄ cup sour cream
- 1 tsp grated horseradish

For the marinade

- 1 cup dry white wine
- ¹/₂ cup olive oil
- 1 large onion, thinly sliced
- 2 cloves garlic, crushed
- 20 black peppercorns
- 2 tsp dried thyme

Make the marinade first. Combine all the marinade ingredients in a large, shallow dish, and blend well. Add the venison to the dish, turn to coat, and set aside to marinate at room temperature for 24 hours. Baste occasionally.

Heat the oven to 450°F. Remove the venison from the marinade, and pat dry with absorbent paper towels. Pour the marinade through a strainer and set it aside.

Using your fingertips, rub the venison all over with salt and pepper. Put it on a rack in a large, deep roasting tin, and arrange the bacon over the top. Pour the reserved marinade and stock into the roasting tin, and place in the preheated oven. Roast for 30 minutes.

Reduce the temperature to 350°F. Cook the venison, basting every 15 minutes, for a further 1¹/₄–1¹/₂ hours until it is tender.

Remove the venison from the oven and transfer to a carving board; discard the bacon. Pour the pan liquid into a small saucepan and bring to the boil over high heat. Reduce to low and stir in the sour cream and horseradish. Simmer for a couple of minutes until the sauce is warm. Transfer to a warmed sauceboat.

Carve the venison into thick slices and arrange on a platter. Serve immediately with the sauce.

DESSERT FRUIT DRINK

KISEL

◆ ◆ ◆

**Kisel is a traditional summer dessert, changing its
character as the different fruits come into season.
It can also be thinned to become a sweet drink, a summer
treat in the days before colas and other carbonated drinks
became the norm, even in Russia.**

SERVES 4–6

- 1 lb raspberries, strawberries, blueberries, cherries, peeled apricots, or peaches
- 2¹/₂ cups water
- ¹/₂ cup sugar
- 2–2¹/₂ tbsp arrowroot
- ²/₃ cup white or red wine (optional)

Place the washed and cleaned fruit into a saucepan with the water. Bring to the boil, then simmer for 15–20 minutes. The fruit should be very pulpy. Strain the liquid from the fruit into a bowl. Be careful not to press on the fruit too hard; it will make the juice cloudy.

Discard the solids and return the juice to the saucepan, together with the sugar. Bring to the boil, then lower the heat and simmer. In a small bowl, whisk the arrowroot with 4 tbsp of the juice (use 2 tbsp arrowroot if not including the wine; otherwise, add 2¹/₂ tbsp). Stir the thickening into the juice and the wine, if using. Continue to simmer, whisking, for a few minutes. Remove from the heat, cool slightly, pour into individual glasses, and chill for at least 4 hours before serving.

APPLE CHARLOTTE, RUSSIAN-STYLE

CHARLOTTKA

◆ ◆ ◆

This famous dessert was the creation of Anton Carême, chef to Tsar Alexander I in the first quarter of the 19th century. The great French cook exploited the Russian love of fruit purées – *charlottkas* usually have apple or soft fruit fillings or accompanying sauces. This popular version makes use of apricot custard.

SERVES 8–9

- ◆ *1–2 tbsp apricot jam*
- ◆ *16–18 sponge fingers*
- ◆ *²/₃ cup whipping or heavy cream*
- ◆ *4 oz can baby mandarin segments, drained*

For the custard filling

- ◆ *1 lb can apricot halves in syrup, drained and syrup reserved*
- ◆ *5 tsp gelatine*
- ◆ *8 egg yolks*
- ◆ *¹/₂ cup sugar*
- ◆ *1¹/₄ cups milk*
- ◆ *³/₄ cup heavy cream*
- ◆ *¹/₂ cup sour cream*
- ◆ *90 ml/6 tbsp Cointreau, Grand Marnier, or other orange liqueur*

Spread the jam thinly around the inside edge of a 8–9 in, deep springform cake pan. Measure the sponge fingers against the sides of the tin, and cut off one end so that they will stand up. Line them up side-to-side, all around the inside of the pan, pressing them into the jam.

Make the purée and custard filling. Place the drained fruit in a blender or a food processor fitted with a metal blade. Add ¹/₂ cup of the apricot syrup, and purée the apricots. Place 3 tbsp apricot syrup in a small bowl, and sprinkle the gelatine into it. Put the bowl into a pan of hot water, and stir the syrup and gelatine until the latter has dissolved.

Beat the egg yolks with the sugar in a bowl placed over a pan of hot water until the mixture is creamy and lemon yellow. Bring the milk to simmering point, and slowly stir it into the egg mixture, stirring all the time. Continue to stir over the hot water until the mixture has become a spoon-coating custard. Stir the gelatine into the custard, take off the heat, and allow to cool to room temperature.

Whisk the apricot purée into the custard, then cover and chill in the refrigerator until the mixture is satiny and just beginning to set. In a bowl, combine the heavy cream and sour cream, and whip until they reach stiff peak stage. Fold into the apricot mixture, together with the orange liqueur.

Pour the mixture into the sponge finger-lined cake pan. Chill for 4 hours or overnight.

To unmold, run a knife around between the pan and the biscuits. Spring open the pan and slip the charlotte out. Whip the whipping or heavy cream, fill a piping bag, and circle the top of the charlotte with piped rosettes. Place a mandarin segment on top of each rosette. Keep chilled until ready to serve.

TEA ICE CREAM WITH RUM SAUCE

CHAINOYE MOROZHENNOYE Z ROMOVOY PODLIVKOY

◆ ◆ ◆

This is an updated version of a dessert once served in the grand salons of Russian nobility. Elegant and light, it from the Silk Road through Central Asia and Caucasia

SERVES 8

- ◆ $^1/_4$ lb kumquats, trimmed and finely chopped
- ◆ $^1/_2$ cup granulated sugar
- ◆ 2 tbsp water
- ◆ 2 tbsp shelled pistachios
- ◆ 5 tbsp black tea leaves
- ◆ 6 tbsp boiling water
- ◆ 5 large egg yolks
- ◆ 1$^1/_2$ cup heavy cream
- ◆ 3 large egg whites
- ◆ $^1/_3$ cup plus 1 tbsp powdered sugar

For the topping

- ◆ 2 tbsp powdered sugar
- ◆ 1 tbsp golden rum
- ◆ $^1/_2$ cup chilled heavy cream

In a small saucepan, combine the kumquats with half the granulated sugar and the water. Bring to the boil, stirring, then lower the heat and simmer, stirring frequently until the kumquats are pulpy. Let the mixture cool, and drain off the excess liquid.

Pour boiling water over the pistachios and leave for 1 minute. Drain and rub off the skins.

Place the boiling water in a bowl and add 2 tbsp tea leaves. Leave to stand for 3 minutes, then strain into another bowl. Press the leaves with a spoon to extract all the juice.

In a small saucepan, mix together the steeped tea and the remaining granulated sugar. Bring to the boil, and stir until the sugar is dissolved and the syrup is shiny and thickening, or measures 120°F on a sugar thermometer.

Meanwhile, beat the egg yolks in a bowl until they are thick and lemon-colored. Pour in the tea syrup little by little, beating constantly, until the mixture has cooled.

In a saucepan, heat $^1/_2$ cup cream until it boils, remove from the heat, and stir in the remaining tea leaves. Leave to stand for 5 minutes, then strain into a bowl, pressing hard with the back of a spoon to extract all the juice. Whisk together the tea-cream and the egg yolk mixture.

In another bowl, beat the egg whites until they reach soft peaks, then beat in the powdered sugar until they become stiff. Fold the meringue into the tea-cream and egg yolk mixture.

In another bowl, beat the remaining cream until it reaches soft peak stage. Fold into the tea-cream mixture with the pistachios.

Line a 1$^1/_2$ quart bombe mold with plastic wrap. Spoon the drained kumquats into the bottom of the bombe mold, pressing up around the sides as far as they will go. Pour the tea-cream mixture into the mold, and smooth the top. Freeze for at least 4 hours, or until it is solid.

Meanwhile, make the rum topping. Beat the rum and the sugar until the sugar has dissolved. Add the cream, and continue to beat until the mixture has thickened. Serve the unmolded ice cream with the rum sauce.

SOFT SWEET CHEESE PANCAKES

TVOROZHNIKI

◆ ◆ ◆

These hand-formed pancakes are sometimes served for breakfast in the better Moscow and St. Petersburg hotels. The constituents bear a distinct resemblance to the fillings you will find in later chapters – the combination of lemon rind, eggs, and cheese is well-loved throughout Eastern Europe and Western Russia.

SERVES 4–6

- ◆ $^1/_2$ cup plain flour
- ◆ 1 lb curd cheese
- ◆ 1 large egg
- ◆ salt
- ◆ 1 tbsp sugar
- ◆ $^1/_2$ tsp vanilla essence
- ◆ grated rind of 1 small lemon
- ◆ flour
- ◆ 3 tbsp–$^1/_4$ cup butter
- ◆ sour cream (optional)
- ◆ fresh fruit – apricots, peaches, raspberries, as desired (optional)

Sieve the flour into a large bowl, then force the curd cheese through the same sieve into the bowl. Add the egg, a pinch of salt, the sugar, vanilla essence, and lemon rind. Stir to mix well.

Transfer the mixture to a floured board and form into 12 small patties. Arrange on a plate, cover with plastic wrap, and chill for 2–24 hours.

Before cooking, dredge the patties in flour, brushing off the excess. Melt the butter in a frying pan and cook the *tvorzhniki* until they are golden brown on both sides. Serve warm with sour cream, and fresh soft fruit, peeled and sliced, if desired.

2

FROM RUSSIA'S HEARTLAND
The Russian Federation

THE NEWLY CHRISTENED RUSSIAN FEDERATION
ENCOMPASSES THE SAME VAST AREA ONCE KNOWN AS
THE RUSSIAN REPUBLIC. ITS VERTICAL EXPANSE STRETCHES
FROM THE ICY TUNDRA OF ARCTIC SIBERIA TO THE SOUTHERN
SHORES OF LAKE BAIKAL.
A CROW FLYING EAST TO WEST WOULD CROSS
FIVE TIME ZONES.

"If we have bread and *kvas*, what more do we need?" So says the anonymous peasant of Russian folklore. This was likely to have been a stoical acceptance of the poor man's lot rather than an out-of-hand rejection of improvement, since the chances of much else in medieval to 19th-century Russia were limited.

Black, brown, or white bread was the staple, served up in thick chunks, and also used in stuffings, soups and, together with barley or rye flour, as the basis for *kvas* (near beer), a Slavic invention.

Some trademarks of European Russian cuisine had come with the invasion of the Tartars – sour cream and curd cheese, fruit relishes and conserves, cucumbers and cabbage preserved in brine, and tea. In general, however, medieval to 19th-century peasant cuisine evolved around the need to cook with very little or no meat – for the most part a luxury reserved for Orthodox feast days.

In addition to wheat and rye flour breads – often eaten with cloves of garlic and coarse salt – the countryman's larder relied on grains and vegetables that would survive the long winters in earth cellars or on the shelf: salted or pickled cabbage, swedes, buckwheat flour and groats (*kasha*), barley (*yachmyer*), millet (*prosso*), onions, beets and potatoes – the latter brought to Russia at the instigation of Peter the Great. Fresh items might include eggs, sour cream (*smetana*), homemade pot cheese, wild soft fruits, and mushrooms. These last are still an obsession with Russians today.

PRE-REVOLUTIONARY RUSSIA

With the Great Reforms of the 1860s, serfs were freed, the lot of the small landowner improved, and village communes were set up. By the late 19th century, Russia and the Ukraine were exporting wheat to a needy Europe. The physical limitations imposed by the size of the country, the corruption of officialdom, and the intransigence of the class system would eventually combine with other political factors to bring about revolution, but for the first time in many homes there was meat in the pot, if only poorer cuts which could be minced or stewed while the better ones went to market. For this reason the Russian tradition of peasant cookery is particularly rich in recipes for leafy vegetables, dumplings and pastries stuffed with meat, as well as for meatballs, patties, and rissoles.

TRADITIONAL SOUPS

Perhaps the greatest culinary contribution of the Russian peasantry, however, is the repertoire of wonderful comfort soups originally made to sustain laborers and farmers during the long cold winters, and of light, chilled soups devised to bring refreshment in the hottest of humid summers. Many exhibit an idiosyncratic sour tang provided by adding pickles, capers, lemon juice, vinegar, *kvas*, sour cream, sorrel, or sauerkraut, while a strongly flavored meat and vegetable stock acts as a foil. Typically, ingredients, too, have body – barley or hunks of bread, chunky pieces of potato, beet, cabbage, and cheaper cuts of meat thicken the broth of winter soups, while finely chopped or puréed vegetables, wild mushrooms – fresh or dried – greens, and, sometimes, fruits form the basis of summer specialties.

Though the grand tradition of cooking – as described in the previous chapter – was evolving into a comfortable bourgeois cuisine by the beginning of the 20th century, the revolution of 1917 brought

an end to that. The peasant diet became the only ideologically acceptable one. Of all the Soviet states, it was probably Russia itself that suffered most in its self-imposed gustatory *gulag*.

The wholesome, if basic, Russian peasant cuisine, if treated with respect, could have developed like the cooking traditions of nearby Germany, Poland, and Hungary. Certainly its Russo-Slavic foundation was rich in leavening influences even within the republic's borders: from the Cossack, Tartar, and Turkic peoples of the lower Volga-Don and northern Transcaucasian regions; from the Karelians (relatives of the Finns) in the north; from the eclectic mixture of indigenous and exiled races in Siberia. But circumstances of history and economics conspired to make that scenario impossible.

PERESTROIKA IN THE KITCHEN

The lack of coherent development strategy in farming and technology, the emphasis on ideology in place of imagination, the stark realities of survival under successive repressive regimes, all meant that cultivated frivolities like cooking and eating well were not, could not, be of interest. In effect, European Russian cooking has been on the back burner – with the gas turned off – since 1917. But *perestroika* (restructuring) has come to the kitchen as well, and now almost three-quarters of a century of neglect is finally being countered by new interest in foodie capitals abroad, and in the cooperative restaurants springing up in Russian cities. It will take time, but the pride in heritage exhibited by these exclusive establishments will find its way back to a people who can now plan for the future while freely talking of the past.

Above: *On the Khabesky state farm, shepherds tend their flock on the northern slope of the Greater Caucasus.*

Far Left: *In a huge commercial greenhouse in the Stavropol region of Russia, a worker sorts red peppers.*

Below: *Harvesting wheat on a collective farm in the Belgorod region of Russia*

COLD VEGETABLE, MEAT, AND KVAS SOUP

OKROSHKA

◆ ◆ ◆

The *kvas* can be replaced by flat beer or semi-sweet cider, though the slightly sour flavor of rye will be missing. This dish may be served hot or cold.

SERVES 6–8

- ◆ *2 hard-boiled eggs, separated*
- ◆ *2 tsp dry mustard powder*
- ◆ *$^2/_3$ cup sour cream*
- ◆ *salt and freshly ground black pepper*
- ◆ *$5^1/_3$ cup* kvas, *flat beer, or cider*
- ◆ *1 medium cucumber, peeled, seeded, and finely diced*

- ◆ *2 scallions, including trimmed green top, finely chopped*
- ◆ *2 medium potatoes, cooked, peeled, and finely diced*
- ◆ *$^1/_2$ lb cold cooked roast beef or pork, finely diced*
- ◆ *large pinch of cayenne pepper*
- ◆ *3 tbsp dill or chives, finely chopped*

Finely chop the whites of the eggs and set aside. In a bowl, mash the yolks with the dry mustard powder and a teaspoonful of the sour cream until you have a paste. Then slowly whip in the rest of the sour cream until smooth. Season with $1^1/_2$–2 tsp salt and pepper to taste.

Whisk in the *kvas*, little by little, until the liquid is thoroughly combined with the sour cream mixture. Stir in the egg whites, cucumber, onions, potatoes, meat, and cayenne pepper. Chill for 15 minutes, then ladle into bowls and garnish with chopped dill or chives.

BORSCH

• • •

To most people, borsch is the quintessential Russian dish. It appears in countless variations: clear and chilled for the summer, with a variety of meats in Ukrainian or Moldovan manner, or with the addition of less orthodox ingredients, such as mushrooms or barley.

SERVES 6

- 2–3 tbsp butter
- 2 beef shins, cut into thin slices
- 1 large onion, chopped
- 1 medium turnip, chopped
- 1 large carrot, sliced
- 2 lb fresh beets, diced
- 8³/₄ cups beef stock
- 4 tbsp red wine vinegar
- 2 bay leaves
- 1 tsp sugar
- salt and freshly ground black pepper
- 5 sprigs fresh parsley
- 5 sprigs fresh dill
- ¹/₂ lb white cabbage, cored and shredded
- 1 cup sour cream

In a large saucepan, melt the butter over medium heat and add the meat, onion, turnip, and carrot. Cook briefly, tossing the meat and vegetables, for about 10 minutes, until the meat is browned and the vegetables softened and sweated. Stir in the beets and 1 cup of the beef stock, the vinegar, bay leaves, sugar, and seasoning to taste. The soup will need quite a bit of salt to bring out the flavor, so don't be too stingy; about 1¹/₂ tsp should be about right. Cover the pan, and simmer the contents for 45 minutes.

Uncover the pan and add the parsley and dill, tied together, and the shredded cabbage, along with the rest of the beef stock. Bring to the boil, then cover and simmer for another 30 minutes.

Before serving, remove the bundle of herbs and the bay leaves. Stir the soup, breaking up the meat and mashing some of the vegetables for a thicker consistency. Serve the soup in warmed bowls, and top each with a tablespoon of sour cream.

KVAS

Recipes for this vary slightly in how sweet they are. Start with this slightly tarter recipe, and increase the amount of sugar if desired. This is sold by street vendors and taken as a cold drink with meals, but it will probably find more favor with American cooks as an ingredient for cold summer soups.

MAKES ABOUT 3 QUARTS

- 1 lb slightly stale black or dark rye bread
- 3 quarts boiling water
- 5 tsp/(2 x ¹/₄ oz packets) active dry yeast
- ¹/₂ cup sugar
- 3 tbsp lukewarm water
- 1 large sprig of mint
- sultanas or raisins

Preheat the oven to 225°F. Place the bread in the oven for about 1–1¹/₂ hours, or until it is very dry. *Do not let it burn.* Crumble the bread into a bowl, and pour the boiling water over it. Cover with a tea towel, and leave for at least 8 hours.

Line a fine sieve with cheesecloth and strain the bread liquid through it into a large bowl, pressing the bread with a spoon to extract as much liquid as possible. Discard the bread.

Sprinkle the yeast and a large pinch of sugar over the lukewarm water, and stir to dissolve completely. Set aside in a warm spot for about 10 minutes, or until the mixture is foamy and almost double in volume. Stir the yeast mixture, the rest of the sugar, and the mint sprig into the bread water. Cover with a tea towel and set aside for another 8–12 hours.

Strain the liquid again through a cheesecloth-lined sieve placed over a large bowl. Sterilize 3 x 1 quart bottles – glass juice bottles will do well. Pour the liquid into each bottle until it is about two-thirds full, then drop in 4–5 raisins or sultanas. Cover the tops with plastic wrap secured with a rubber band.

Place the bottles in a cool, dark place for about 3 days, until the raisins/sultanas have risen to the top and the sediment sunk to the bottom. Carefully pour off the clear liquid into a bowl, leaving the sediment behind. Thoroughly clean the bottles, remove the raisins/sultanas from the *kvas*, and funnel it back into the bottles (there will be slightly less than before). Cork the bottles or cover with plastic wrap and refrigerate until ready to use. The *kvas* will keep for several weeks if kept well-covered in the fridge.

SIBERIAN MEAT DUMPLINGS

PELMENI

◆ ◆ ◆

Traditionally, *pelmeni* were made in the autumn, with the coming of the first snowfalls. They were frozen, uncooked, in the snow banks outside the house, and hacked off in chunks whenever needed. The fillings used off-cuts of meat, while the dough could be made with or without egg. For fish *pelmeni*, substitute halibut, bream, or salmon for the meat, and butter mashed with two hard-boiled egg yolks for the pork fat.

MAKES ABOUT 65–70

◆ *2 cups plain flour*
◆ *salt*
◆ *1 large egg*

◆ *melted butter (optional)*
◆ *sour cream (optional)*

For the filling

◆ *6 oz lean ground beef*
◆ *¹/₄ lb finely chopped lean pork*
◆ *2 oz finely chopped pork fat*

◆ *1 large onion, finely chopped*
◆ *1 tsp salt*
◆ *freshly ground black pepper*

To make the filling, mix together all the filling ingredients in a large bowl. Set aside.

To make the dough, place the flour and salt in the bowl of a food processor fitted with a metal blade. With the motor running, add the egg, then as much water as is necessary for the dough to just begin to form a ball (about 2–4 tbsp). Remove the dough, and place on a floured surface. Knead for about 8 minutes or until smooth, flouring the surface as necessary to keep the dough from sticking. Form the dough back into a ball, flatten slightly, and chill it, wrapped in plastic wrap, for about 2 hours.

To make the *pelmeni*, roll out the dough on a lightly floured surface until it is a rectangle about ¹/₈ in thick. Place your fists under the dough and begin stretching it by pulling it carefully over the backs of your hands. When it is very thin, spread it on a table. With a knife, trim it into a square or rectangle, and cut out 3 in rounds with a cookie cutter or lid. Drop a scant 1 tsp of filling on one side of each round. Brush the circular edge all around with a little water, and fold the dough over to form a half circle. Seal by pressing the edges with a fork. Wet both ends of the *pelmeni*, bring them around, and pinch together in the shape of an Italian tortellini. Arrange the *pelmeni* on a baking tray, cover with a tea towel, and freeze overnight. (The *pelmeni* may be kept frozen for up to 3 months.)

To cook the *pelmeni*, bring 8 cups water to the boil in a large saucepan. Drop the *pelmeni* in by the dozen, bring back to the boil, and reduce the heat to low. Simmer uncovered for about 10 minutes, or until they rise to the surface. Remove with a slotted spoon, drain thoroughly, and bring the water back to the boil. Repeat with the remaining *pelmeni*. Serve with melted butter or sour cream.

PRETZEL-SHAPED SWEET BREAD

KRENDEL

◆ ◆ ◆

This much-loved sweet bread makes a delicious accompaniment to tea drawn from a silver samovar. Given a more cake-like consistency with the addition of more flour and eggs, but retaining the same shape, it is also popular as the centerpiece for a birthday or name-day celebration.

MAKES 1 LOAF

◆ *3 tbsp lukewarm water*
◆ *2¹/₂ tsp (1 x ¹/₄ oz packet) active dry yeast*
◆ *3 tbsp plus 1 tsp sugar*
◆ *3 cups plain flour*
◆ *¹/₂ tsp salt*

◆ *¹/₄ cup unsalted butter*
◆ *scant ¹/₂ cup slivered blanched almonds*
◆ *3 eggs*
◆ *¹/₂ cup light cream*
◆ *2 tbsp powdered sugar*

Place the lukewarm water in a small bowl, and sprinkle in the yeast and 1 tsp sugar. Leave for 10 minutes to become foamy and almost double in volume.

Sift 300 g/11 oz of the flour, the remaining sugar, and the salt into another bowl. Cut in the butter in small pieces, and work the mixture with your hands until it becomes crumbly. Lightly beat 2 eggs and stir into the flour mixture, followed by the cream and the yeast mixture. Combine thoroughly to make a dough. If the dough is not firm enough, sift in the remaining flour, little by little, until the dough is manageable.

Gather the dough into a ball and transfer to a well-floured surface. Knead for about 5 minutes, or until it is smooth and elastic. Reshape into a ball, transfer to a lightly buttered bowl, turn the dough to coat in the butter, cover with a tea towel, and let it rise for 30 minutes or until double in size.

Knock down the dough and, on a floured surface, shape it into a long rope about 2 in in diameter. Taper the ends and twist the dough over and under into a pretzel shape.

Preheat the oven to 400°F. Transfer the dough to a buttered baking tray, cover again with the tea towel, and leave to rise in a warm place until it has doubled in size, about 30 minutes. Brush with an egg wash made from beating the remaining egg with a little water, and sprinkle with the almonds.

Bake for 15 minutes, then cover with foil and bake for 10–15 minutes more, until the top and almonds are golden. Transfer the bread to a rack and when cool, sprinkle with sifted powdered sugar.

Pretzel-shaped Sweet Bread

MARINATED MUSHROOMS

MARINOVANNYE GRIBY

In Russia, the Ukraine and the Baltic states, some of the enthusiasm for wild mushrooms is now tempered with fear, since fungi – particularly the thick-stalked *cep* or *boletus* known colloquially as the "Penny Bun" – have been shown to be severely contaminated by the fallout from Chernobyl. Fortunately, our own wild mushrooms, and those available from an increasing number of suppliers, are unaffected.

SERVES 4–6

- *1 lb fresh whole button mushrooms, or a mixture of button and oyster mushrooms*
- *2 cloves garlic*
- *2 whole cloves*
- *1 bay leaf*
- *sunflower or vegetable oil*
- *1 tbsp sugar*
- *2 tsp salt*
- *1 cup red wine vinegar*
- *²/₃ cup water*
- *3 peppercorns*

Trim the stalks of the mushrooms so that they are flat with the caps, and remove any discolored parts from the oyster mushrooms. Place the garlic, cloves, bay leaf, peppercorns, sugar, and salt in an enamelled or stainless steel saucepan, and cover with vinegar and water. Bring the liquid to the boil, add the mushrooms, and reduce the heat. Simmer uncovered for about 20 minutes, until the mushrooms sink to the bottom. Remove from the heat, take out the garlic, and let the mixture cool.

Pour the mushrooms and their liquid into quart jars, and pour just enough oil over to create a film on top. Cover with plastic wrap secured with rubber bands, and refrigerate for at least 10 days before using. (They should keep for several months if refrigerated.)

MEATBALLS WITH CRANBERRY SAUCE

◆ ◆ ◆
BITKI

These tasty little patties can be made with either beef or pork – the latter is probably more common in western Russia and the Ukraine. While the recipe offers the option of cranberry jelly as an accompaniment, in its home regions *bitki* would more usually be paired with lingonberries.

SERVES 4–5

- ◆ $^1/_4$ *cup butter*
- ◆ *1 medium onion, finely chopped*
- ◆ *1$^1/_2$ lb ground lean pork or beef*
- ◆ $^1/_2$ *lb ground lean veal*
- ◆ *2 oz finely chopped fresh pork fat*
- ◆ *1 large egg, beaten*
- ◆ *salt and freshly ground black pepper*
- ◆ $^1/_3$ *cup shortening, chicken fat, or dripping*
- ◆ $^2/_3$ *cup sour cream (optional)*
- ◆ $^2/_3$ *cup dry breadcrumbs*
- ◆ $^1/_2$ *cup cranberry jelly (optional)*

Heat the butter over medium heat and add the onions. Cook, stirring occasionally, until lightly colored and softened, about 8 minutes. Transfer to a large bowl and add the ground meats, fat, $^1/_2$ cup breadcrumbs, egg, and seasoning to taste. Work with your hands until all the ingredients are well combined.

Form the *bitki* into 8–10 thick patties. Turn each of the patties over in the remaining breadcrumbs to coat them. Melt half the lard, chicken fat, or dripping in a frying pan over high heat. Fry the patties until they are golden brown, about 5 minutes a side. Transfer to a serving dish and keep warm. Repeat with the remaining lard and patties.

Serve the *bitki* in either of two ways: sour cream can be stirred into the frying pan after the patties are finished, warmed through, and then poured over the *bitki*. Alternatively, serve the *bitki* plain, accompanied by a sauceboat of cranberry jelly.

RUSSIAN-STYLE POTATO SALAD

KARTOPHELNY SALAT PO-RUSSKI

◆ ◆ ◆

This delicious salad incorporates the dressing which has now become internationally known as "Russian Dressing."

SERVES 6–8

- ◆ *2 lb baby potatoes*
- ◆ *2 tbsp finely chopped scallions*
- ◆ *3 tbsp finely chopped fresh dill*
- ◆ *6 tbsp finely chopped sweet-sour pickle*
- ◆ *6 radishes, thinly sliced*
- ◆ *fresh dill sprigs*

For the dressing

- ◆ $^3/_4$ *cup mayonnaise*
- ◆ $^1/_2$ *tsp Worcestershire sauce*
- ◆ *1$^1/_2$ tbsp ketchup*
- ◆ *2 tbsp dry white wine*
- ◆ *1 tsp horseradish sauce*

Put the potatoes in a large saucepan of water and bring to the boil. Cover, lower the heat, and simmer for about 20 – 25 minutes, or until the potatoes are done. Drain and when cool, cut into $^1/_4$ in slices.

In a small bowl, whisk together the ingredients for the dressing. In a large bowl, assemble the potatoes, onion, dill, pickle and radishes. Pour the dressing over, and toss gently to combine. Transfer the salad to a serving bowl, and chill for 30 minutes before serving garnished with the dill sprigs.

FRESH WATER FISH IN MUSTARD SAUCE

OMUL Z ZAPRVKOI GORCHICHINOI

◆ ◆ ◆

Omul is a delicious relative of the salmon, found only in Siberia's Lake Baikal, one of the most beautiful lakes and on record as the deepest (1 mile) in the world.
This recipe would use local wildflower honey, and the fish would be baked over an open brushwood fire; here we must be content with ordinary honey, best king salmon, and a barbecue or grill.

SERVES 6

- ◆ *2 tbsp sunflower oil*
- ◆ *3 lb salmon fillet, washed and dried*
- ◆ *2¹/₂ tbsp German-style mustard*
- ◆ *1¹/₂ tbsp honey*
- ◆ *grated rind and juice of ¹/₂ small lemon*
- ◆ *1 tbsp finely chopped fresh dill*
- ◆ *salt and freshly ground black pepper*
- ◆ *dill sprigs*

If you are grilling the fish, brush a sheet of foil with a little sunflower oil before placing the salmon skin-side down on it. Whether grilling or barbecueing, place the fish (and foil, if used) on a baking tray. Mix together the remaining oil, mustard, honey, lemon rind and juice, and chopped dill. Brush the fish liberally with the mixture.

Pre-heat a grill to hot. (If you are using a barbecue, the coals should be graying. Place the fish in a fish holder and turn it flesh-side down toward the coals.)

Grill or barbecue the fish about 5 in from the heat for about 10 minutes, or until slightly translucent. Transfer to a serving platter, and garnish with dill sprigs before serving.

Stuffed Cabbage Rolls

Golubtsy

◆ ◆ ◆

Cabbage rolls are made by Russians, Poles, Czechs and Hungarians, though each version has special spices and ingredients. The Hungarian one makes use of paprika, while typical recipes from the Ukraine – where they are called *holubsti* – contain mushrooms and are often meatless.

SERVES 8

- 2$\frac{1}{2}$–3 lb white Dutch or Savoy cabbage
- 3 tbsp butter
- 1 tbsp oil
- 2 large onions, finely chopped
- 1 lb lean ground beef
- $\frac{1}{2}$ lb lean ground veal
- 1 cup cooked long-grain white rice
- 1 egg, beaten
- salt and freshly ground black pepper
- 6 slices bacon
- 14 oz can chopped tomatoes
- $\frac{1}{2}$ cup beef stock
- 1 tbsp flour
- scant $\frac{2}{3}$ cup sour cream
- 3 tbsp plus 1 tsp fresh dill, finely chopped

Bring a large saucepan or casserole of water to boil. Lower in the whole head of cabbage. Cover and cook for about 8 minutes. Remove the cabbage, but keep the water on the boil. Carefully remove as many leaves as you can without tearing them. Return the cabbage head to the saucepan and cook for a little longer, then remove and again detach as many leaves as you can. Repeat the process until you have 20 or so large leaves. Trim each leaf, removing the toughest part of the central stalk. Set aside.

In a frying pan, heat the butter and oil and sauté the onion until it is softened and golden. Transfer to a large bowl and add the beef, veal, cooked rice, egg, and seasoning to taste. Mix with your hands until thoroughly combined.

Lay 3–4 leaves out, and place about 3 tbsp of filling on each. Roll up from the stalk end, turning in the sides, and finish at the leafy end to make a neat packet. If necessary, secure with a wooden cocktail stick. Place the packets seam-side down in a shallow casserole large enough to hold all the rolls in one layer. Lay the bacon slices over the rolls.

Preheat the oven to 350°F. In a saucepan, heat together the chopped tomatoes and beef stock. Remove 2 tbsp to mix with the flour in a bowl. Whisk in the sour cream and dill, and return the mixture to the hot tomato-beef stock mixture, stirring all the while as you do so. Season to taste, and pour the sauce over the cabbage rolls.

Bake the rolls, uncovered, for 1 hour or until the sauce is bubbling and the rolls are slightly browned. Allow to rest for 10 minutes before serving.

HAM SAUSAGE WITH CABBAGE

KOLBASA Z KAPUSTOY

◆ ◆ ◆

Kolbasa **is a smoked ham sausage common throughout the European states. Like many processed pork products, it is largely produced for sale in Poland and nearby Ukraine and Belorussia. It can be eaten hot or cold.**

SERVES 4–6

- ◆ *1 large head red cabbage, shredded*
- ◆ *2 tbsp butter*
- ◆ *¹/₃ cup lemon juice*
- ◆ *100 ml/ 4 fl oz beef stock*
- ◆ *50 ml/2 fl oz red wine*
- ◆ *salt and pepper*
- ◆ *2 tsp brown sugar*
- ◆ *1 tbsp cornstarch*
- ◆ *1 lb kolbasa or other smoked ham sausage, thinly sliced*

Place the shredded cabbage in a colander and pour boiling water over it. Drain thoroughly.

Melt the butter in a heavy flameproof casserole over medium heat. Stir in the cabbage and sauté for 5 minutes. Add the lemon juice and continue stirring for another 5 minutes; the cabbage will be bright pink. Pour the stock and wine over it, cover, and lower the heat. Simmer for 45 minutes.

Mix together the sugar and cornstarch in a small bowl; stir in a little of the cooking liquid. Stir the mixture into the cabbage, and raise the heat to high. Stir as the sauce thickens, then add the sausage. Cover and simmer for 30 minutes. Serve with thick slabs of rye bread.

HAM IN RYE PASTRY

OKOROK V RZHANOM TESTE

◆ ◆ ◆

This is a popular Easter dish that can be served either hot or cold, as here. It would be well partnered by cabbage cooked with sour cream, boiled potatoes with dill, and a pot of German-style mustard. The rather hard, dry pastry can be discarded before serving, if desired; it is really there to seal in the flavor of the spiced ham.

SERVES 10–12

- ◆ *¹/₃ cup plus 1 tbsp dark brown sugar*
- ◆ *1 tsp dry mustard powder*
- ◆ *¹/₄ tsp ground cloves*
- ◆ *large pinch of ground cinnamon*
- ◆ *5 lb canned Polish ham*
- ◆ *milk*

For the pastry

- ◆ *2¹/₂ tsp (1 x ¹/₄ oz packet) active dry yeast*
- ◆ *3 tbsp lukewarm water*
- ◆ *4 tbsp caraway seeds*
- ◆ *³/₄ cup water*
- ◆ *2 tbsp molasses*
- ◆ *3 cups rye flour*

Make the pastry first. Dissolve the yeast in lukewarm water in a small bowl. Add the caraway seeds, and set aside in a warm place for 10 minutes to become foamy and double in volume.

Stir in ³/₄ cup cold water, the molasses and half the flour, a little at a time. Take the resultant dough out of the bowl, and place on a floured surface. Knead in the remaining flour, little by little. The dough should be stiff. Cover with plastic wrap and set aside for 30 minutes. Meanwhile, remove the aspic from the ham, and pat the ham dry with absorbent paper towels.

Roll out the dough to form a 26 x 10 in rectangle. Mix together the sugar, mustard, cloves, and cinnamon in a small bowl. Sprinkle a heaped tablespoon of the mixture in the center of the dough. Place the ham on top, and pat the remaining mixture over the ham.

Preheat the oven to 350°F. Fold the dough neatly over the ham, tucking the corners in and sealing it where the edges meet with a little water. Set the ham on a foil-lined baking tray, brush with milk, and bake for 1³/₄–2 hours. Remove from the oven and allow to rest for 15 minutes before slicing the ham (and removing the pastry surround, if desired).

Ham Sausage with Cabbage

DEEP-FRIED BUTTER TWISTS

KHVOROST

◆ ◆ ◆

These are among the most beloved of Russian cookies. They are a happy reminder of childhood to many Russian immigrants around the world.

MAKES ABOUT 25–30

◆ *1 large egg*
◆ *4 large egg yolks*
◆ *4 tbsp powdered sugar*
◆ *2 tbsp rum*
◆ *1 tsp vanilla essence*
◆ *¹/₂ tsp salt*
◆ *²/₃ cup plain flour*
◆ *oil or fat*
◆ *powdered sugar, or combination of granulated sugar and ground cinnamon*

In a large bowl, use an electric mixer to beat the egg and egg yolks with the sugar until the mixture is thick and fluffy – about 10 minutes. Stir in the rum, vanilla essence, and salt.

Sift the flour into the bowl little by little, stirring after each addition. By the time you have added ²/₃ cup, you should have a stiff paste; turn it out on to a floured surface. Knead the dough on a floured surface until smooth and elastic – about 10 minutes. Divide the dough in half, and cover half with a damp towel.

Roll out the dough as thinly as possible, and cut into 5 x 2 in strips. Make a slit from the center almost to the end of one strip, and thread the other end through the slit. Repeat with the remaining strips. Roll out the remaining dough and repeat the process.

Heat the oil or fat in a deep-fryer or large saucepan until water-spit hot, and deep-fry the *khvorost*, turning once or twice, in batches, until golden. Drain the twists on paper towels before sprinkling with cinnamon powdered sugar.

RUSSIAN-STYLE CHEESE CAKE

VATRUSHKI

◆ ◆ ◆

***Vatrushki* are served as a savory *zakuska*, as a sweet to go with tea, as here, or as a large dessert tart.**

MAKES ABOUT 16 TARTLETS

- ◆ 1³/₄ cup plain flour
- ◆ ¹/₂ tsp baking powder
- ◆ ¹/₄ cup sugar
- ◆ pinch of salt

- ◆ 1 large egg
- ◆ ¹/₃ cup plus 1 tbsp sour cream
- ◆ ¹/₄ cup unsalted butter

For the filling

- ◆ ¹/₄ cup rum
- ◆ 2 tbsp water
- ◆ ¹/₂ cup raisins
- ◆ 1 cup plus 2 tbsp cottage cheese
- ◆ 4 eggs

- ◆ ³/₄ cup sugar
- ◆ 2 tsp grated lemon rind
- ◆ ¹/₂ cup clarified butter, melted
- ◆ ¹/₄ tsp salt
- ◆ ¹/₂ cup flour

Make the filling first. Heat the rum and 2 tbsp water in a saucepan over high heat until almost boiling. Remove from the heat and stir in the raisins. Set aside.

Line a colander with cheesecloth and pour in the cottage cheese. Leave to drain for 3 hours.

In a large bowl, beat the cottage cheese using an electric mixer. Beat in the eggs, one at a time, and the sugar, until the mixture is pale in color. Stir in the lemon rind, melted butter, salt and flour, 1 tbsp at a time. Drain the raisins, discard the liquid, and fold the raisins into the cottage cheese.

To make the dough, sift the flour, baking powder, sugar, and salt into a large bowl. Beat the egg and sour cream in a small bowl. Make a well in the center of the flour and pour the egg mixture into it. With your hands, slowly work the flour into the liquid, then beat until the mixture forms a ball. Wrap in plastic wrap and chill for 1 hour.

Preheat the oven to 400°F. On a well-floured surface, roll the dough out into a rectangle as thinly as possible. Cut out 16 or so 4 in rounds from the dough, gathering and rerolling the scraps as necessary. Make a rim around each circle by folding over and pinching up the dough, so that you end up with shallow tartlet cases.

Place the cases on a greased baking tray, and spoon some of the filling into each case. Bake for 15–20 minutes, or until the *vatrushki* are golden. Remove and cool on a wire rack.

WHIPPED EGGS AND SUGAR

GOGOL MOGOL

◆ ◆ ◆

This is Russian *zabaglione*, simple as that!
A timeless dessert, made in kitchens all over Russia.

SERVES 2–3

◆ *6 egg yolks* ◆ *6 tbsp sugar*
◆ *2 tbsp rum*

Beat the sugar with the egg yolk until foamy and pale lemon in color. Stir in the rum. Pour the mixture into tall glasses, and serve with thin, Belgian-style butter twists or *khvorost*.

EASTER CAKE

KULICH

◆ ◆ ◆

**This is the traditional festive Easter cake.
Some recipes include curd cheese to give it a thicker,
pastier consistency.**

SERVES 8–10

- ◆ 2¹/₂ tbsp (3 x ¹/₄ oz packets) active dry yeast
- ◆ 1 cup sugar
- ◆ 2 tsp water
- ◆ ²/₃ cup sultanas
- ◆ ¹/₂ pt lukewarm milk
- ◆ 2 fl oz rum
- ◆ 5–5¹/₂ cups flour
- ◆ ¹/₂ tsp powdered saffron
- ◆ 3 eggs
- ◆ 2 egg yolks
- ◆ 1 tsp vanilla essence
- ◆ ¹/₂ cup unsalted butter, cut into small pieces
- ◆ ¹/₂ cup plus 1 heaped tbsp mixed peel
- ◆ scant ¹/₂ cup slivered almonds, toasted
- ◆ 2 cardomom seeds, crushed to powder
- ◆ flour

For the glaze

- ◆ 1³/₄ cup plus 2 tbsp powdered sugar
- ◆ 2 tsp red wine
- ◆ 7 tsp water

Mix the yeast and 1 tsp sugar with the water to make a paste. Soak the sultanas in the rum for at least 15 minutes.

Stir the lukewarm milk into the yeast paste, and beat in about 2 cups of the flour, until you have a thin batter. Cover and leave in a warm place for 30 minutes to double in volume and become frothy.

Drain the sultanas, reserving the liquid, and pat them dry with paper towel. Add the saffron to the rum and set aside.

Sift the remaining sugar and flour, a little at a time, into the frothy mixture, until you have a stiff batter. Beat the eggs and the egg yolks one at a time into the dough, together with the vanilla essence, kneading with your hands when it becomes possible. Work the butter into the dough little by little.

Pour the saffron and rum over the dough and knead in. Make the dough into a ball and transfer to a floured surface. Knead hard with the heel of your hand, turning and pulling, for about 10 minutes. If necessary, knead in more flour to make sure the dough does not stick. When the dough is shiny and smooth, make into a ball again. Dust with flour, and place in a buttered bowl.

Leave to stand in a warm place for 1 hour, or until the dough has doubled in size.

Toss the mixed peel, slivered almonds, and the soaked and drained sultanas in a bowl with 1 tbsp flour and the crushed cardomom. Knock down the dough in the bowl. Add a little of the mixed fruit and knead in; continue until all the fruit is evenly taken in by the dough. Leave the dough in the bowl, cover it, and put in a warm place for 1 hour to rise again.

Butter a deep cylindrical pan – an empty 2 lb coffee can will do – and line with a buttered piece of waxed paper. When the dough has doubled in size again, knock it down and transfer it to the pan.

Preheat the oven to 400°F. Leave the dough to rise until it almost reaches the top of the pan. Bake for 15 minutes, then lower the heat to 350°F and bake for a further hour, or until the puffed top has turned golden.

Cool in the pan on a wire rack for 10 minutes, then lift carefully, turn out the cake, and cover with a towel. Make the glaze. In a bowl, beat together the powdered sugar, water and red wine with a wooden spoon, until thoroughly combined. Uncover the cake and pour the glaze over it.

Serve by cleanly cutting off the crown and reserving it to be eaten last, then cutting the cake in half vertically and cutting each half into half-circle slices.

LOOKING WESTWARD FROM THE BALTIC

Estonia, Latvia, and Lithuania

THE POLITICAL EVENTS OF THE LAST FIVE TO SIX YEARS HAVE BROUGHT THREE SMALL STATES DRAMATICALLY INTO THE PUBLIC EYE — THREE STATES WHICH MANY IN THE WEST COULD HARDLY LOCATE ON A MAP, MUCH LESS ARRANGE IN GEOGRAPHICAL ORDER DOWN THEIR JAGGED STRETCH OF BALTIC COASTLINE.

This solemn liturgy at Phyti convent is being officiated by Metropolitan Alexiy, who heads 84 Russian Orthodox parishes in Estonia.

Estonia, Latvia, and Lithuania have a common history of subjugation and exploitation by stronger neighbors. These exploiters have included, in varying permutations, Russia, Germany, Denmark, and Sweden, though Lithuania enjoyed a period of influence and independence with her own Duchy, later brought into a Polish-Lithuanian Commonwealth. All fell in the end, however, to the great Russian bear. The repeated submergence of national identity under a foreign yoke, and their final domination by the Soviet Union, has left its mark on the culinary character of all three countries. At the same time, their fierce desire for liberation, which put them in the vanguard of the new independent order, has ensured that some individual characteristics have managed to survive.

The aspects they share have, not surprisingly, been largely dictated by their location flanking the sea, by their rich agricultural land – making them great producers of barley, oatmeal, and rye – and by their proximity to, and dependence on, the old Soviet Union. Buckwheat (*kasha*) is a staple, and Russian-style dishes like stuffed cabbage, meatballs and ground meat cutlets feature prominently. The love of honey which distinguishes much of the former western and southern Soviet states is echoed here, as is the ubiquitous use of sour cream.

Estonia, the most northerly, exhibits a character somewhat apart from its two neighbors. Unlike the Latvians and Lithuanians, Estonians trace their roots to the Finno-Ugric nation and hence share more cultural, linguistic, and even gastronomic links with the Finns. In addition, the large numbers of Finnish tourists who have always treated the charming Estonian capital, Tallinn, as a long-weekend playground (the ferry from Helsinki takes only four hours) have now grown to a flood, so that the links with that country are ever-growing. Both the variety of smoked and salted fish, and the occasions demanding its appearance, are evocative of Scandinavia, while Finnish specialties like Queen's Cake are served in Tallinn's coffee houses (*korviks*) and cafés. Caraway is the dominant flavoring, and *Viru Valge*, a brand of local vodka, shares with Scandinavian versions a reputation among connoisseurs for exceptional quality.

Latvia, like Estonia, has an almost Viennese appreciation of coffee, and of the pastries to go with it. Its fishing industry, one of the world's richest during the independent years between the wars, was afterwards commandeered by the Soviets to feed the Russian heartland. This meant that its wealth of sea and freshwater fish was largely unavailable to the local people, and thus much of its fine heritage of recipes for fresh and smoked fish have long been unappreciated. Its dairy farmers fared somewhat better, and thickly whipped cream, sour cream, and sour milk figure particularly strongly in Latvian cooking. So, too, do fresh berries – raspberries, cranberries, red- and blackcurrants, whortleberries (wild blueberries) – made into preserves, baked into pastries, and puréed into *kisels*. Fruits such as apple, plum, and grape are transformed into drinks called *kosteili*.

Lithuania, the most westernized of the three, is ironically the most Russian in culinary terms. Garlic is as important there as it is in the Ukraine and the Russian Republic, while Lithuanian sausages – particularly a pork and beef version called *sviezia desra* – are reputed to be the most flavorful in Eastern Europe. Both the potato and apple are treated with special respect; mashed, grated, in dumplings and pastry, the former appears in everything from soups to desserts, while the latter features in sweet biscuits, fritters, tarts, cakes, sauces and candy, as well as combining with potatoes in a savory pudding.

Today all three states are independent, broken free of involvement even in the loose union of the CIS. This resurrection from national death has awoken a deep and emotional pride in their past; repercussions in the already bustling restaurant and café scenes of Tallinn, Riga, and Vilnius cannot be far behind.

This artfully arranged pile of firewood, at the Phyti Russian Orthodox convent in Estonia, is as tall as a three-storied building. The birch logs are used in fireplaces for heating, and as kindling in the cooking stoves.

RASPBERRY SOUP

MALINOVYI SUP

◆ ◆ ◆

This is a favorite summer soup of Estonia, as well as other Baltic and Eastern European states. It is considered a specialty by the restaurants of Tallinn, Estonia's capital. In season, whortleberries – wild blueberries – can be substituted.

SERVES 6

- ◆ *1 1/2 lb raspberries or blueberries*
- ◆ *6 oz redcurrants*
- ◆ *1 3/4 cup water*
- ◆ *1 tbsp cornstarch*
- ◆ *juice and rind of 1/2 lemon*
- ◆ *1/2 - 2/3 cup light brown sugar*
- ◆ *1/2 tsp cinnamon*
- ◆ *1 1/4 cups whipping cream*
- ◆ *2/3 cup sour cream*

Reserve a large handful of berries for garnish. Place the remainder in a liquidizer or processor fitted with a metal blade, and process until the berries are liquified.

Place a fine sieve over an enamelled or stainless-steel saucepan. Press the puréed fruit to extract the seeds, stirring through the sieve in batches until all the liquid has passed through.

Add the water to the strained fruit. Place over high heat and bring to the boil; lower the heat and simmer for 15 minutes. In a small bowl, mix the cornstarch with a little water. Whisk into the soup, turn up the heat, and continue whisking as the soup begins to boil and the soup thickens. Lower the heat, and whisk in the lemon juice and rind, sugar, and cinnamon.

Take off the heat, allow to cool, then chill for several hours or overnight.

Before serving, whisk in the whipping and sour creams. Ladle into individual soup bowls, and garnish each with some of the reserved berries.

CREAM OF BARLEY SOUP

SKABA PUTRA

◆ ◆ ◆

This is a very old recipe, handed down through generations and still popular today. It is a cold summer soup, for that surprisingly warm season. The coastal strip of Latvia is lapped by the northeasterly waves of the Gulf Stream, making the climate slightly milder than that of its Scandinavian neighbors.

SERVES 6

- ◆ *1 lb field or brown mushrooms, finely sliced then chopped*
- ◆ *1/4 cup vegetable oil*
- ◆ *1 large onion, finely chopped*
- ◆ *1 1/2 tbsp tomato paste*
- ◆ *2 tbsp fresh lemon juice*
- ◆ *9 cups chicken stock*
- ◆ *1 cup pearl barley*
- ◆ *salt and freshly ground black pepper*
- ◆ *1 cup buttermilk*
- ◆ *1 cup sour cream*
- ◆ *3 tbsp finely chopped fresh dill*
- ◆ *2 hard-boiled eggs, chopped*
- ◆ *1 Polish-style sweet-sour pickle, finely chopped*

In a large saucepan, sauté the mushrooms in the oil over medium-high heat. Stir until the mushroom juices have evaporated, about 15 minutes. Add the onion and stir until softened, about 8 minutes. Stir in the tomato paste, lemon juice and chicken stock, and bring to the boil over high heat.

Slowly stir in the barley and seasoning to taste. Bring back to the boil, cover, and lower the heat. Simmer until the barley is tender, about 30–40 minutes.

Take the soup off the heat and leave to cool. When it is at room temperature, stir in the buttermilk, sour cream, and dill. Taste and adjust the seasoning. Chill for at least 1 hour (or overnight, covered) before serving.

Ladle the soup into individual serving bowls, and garnish each with the chopped egg and pickle.

HONEY VODKA

KRUPNIKAS

◆ ◆ ◆

Honey is used as a sweetening agent in all of the Baltic countries, but it is perhaps in Lithuania that it reaches its apogee. *Midus* (mead) is one warming, honey-based alcoholic beverage; another is homemade "fire" or honey vodka.

MAKES ABOUT 900 ML / 1 ½ PT

- ◆ 1 vanilla bean
- ◆ large pinch nutmeg
- ◆ 4 strips lemon peel
- ◆ ³/₄ cup water
- ◆ 7 sticks cinnamon
- ◆ 3 whole cloves
- ◆ 1 ½ cups honey
- ◆ 1 ¼ pt vodka

In a large saucepan, combine the vanilla bean, nutmeg, cinnamon, cloves, lemon peel, and water. Bring the water to the boil, and stir in the honey. Bring back to the boil, cover and simmer for 5 minutes.

Remove from the heat and stir in the vodka. The *krupnikas* can be served hot or allowed to cool and then bottled.

Lithuanian Cottage Cheese Bacon Bread

LITHUANIAN COTTAGE CHEESE BACON BREAD

LITOVSKY TWOROZHNY KHLEB Z BECONOM

◆ ◆ ◆

Varske – cottage cheese – and honey are commonly used as baking ingredients in Lithuania. This recipe mixes wholemeal and white flour to give a hint of the sturdier type of bread you will find in the Baltic States.

MAKES 1 LOAF WEIGHT

- *¹/₄ cup vegetable oil*
- *6 oz lean bacon, finely chopped*
- *2 heaped tbsp finely chopped scallions*
- *¹/₄ cup honey*
- *³/₄ cup milk*
- *1 egg*
- *¹/₃ cup cottage cheese*
- *1¹/₄ cup wholewheat flour*
- *1¹/₄ cup strong white flour*
- *2 tsp baking powder*
- *¹/₂ tsp baking soda*
- *scant tsp salt*

In a small saucepan, heat the vegetable oil over medium-high heat. Add the bacon and fry for a few minutes, until the bacon is cooked. Turn down the heat and stir in the chopped scallion, allowing it to wilt slightly. Then add the honey, heat through, and remove from the heat. Beat in the milk, egg, and then the cottage cheese. Blend thoroughly and set aside.

In a large bowl, sift together the two flours, baking powder and soda, and the salt. Make a well and pour in the cottage cheese mixture, beating gently – do not overbeat.

Preheat the oven to 375°F. Scrape the bread dough into a buttered and floured 9 x 5 x 3 in loaf pan. Flatten the top of the loaf with a spatula, and drop the loaf sharply twice on a hard surface to eliminate air pockets. Bake for 45–50 minutes, or until the top is golden brown.

Place the pan on a wire rack to cool for 15 minutes before turning out. Cool completely before serving.

BARLEY BREAD

YACHMENNY KHLEB

◆ ◆ ◆

Barley bread is made from Finland to the Ukraine, and it makes a change from the black and coarse rye breads which otherwise predominate in the countryside. In this Estonian recipe, honey is used to provide a touch of sweetness.

MAKES 2 ROUND LOAVES

- *2¹/₂ tsp (1 x ¹/₄ oz packet) active dry yeast*
- *¹/₄ cup honey*
- *¹/₂ cup lukewarm water*
- *1¹/₂ cups cracked barley*
- *1¹/₂ cups wholewheat flour*
- *2 tsp salt*
- *1¹/₂ cups lukewarm milk*
- *2 tbsp vegetable oil*
- *3 cups strong white flour*
- *1 egg*
- *1 tbsp water*

Dissolve the yeast, together with 1 tbsp honey, in the lukewarm water in a small bowl. Cover the bowl, and place it in a warm place for 20 minutes or until foamy and almost doubled in volume.

Meanwhile, in a blender or food processor fitted with a metal blade, grind the barley in batches as finely as possible.

Transfer to a large bowl and add the wholewheat flour and salt. Slowly beat in the yeast mixture, the remaining honey, the lukewarm milk, and the oil. Add as much of the white flour as is needed to make a soft, malleable dough. Remove the dough to a floured surface, and, adding a little more white flour all the time, knead until it is shiny and elastic, about 10 minutes. Remove to a lightly oiled bowl, cover with a tea towel, and allow to rise in a warm place for 1 hour, or until doubled in size.

Knock down the dough, knead for another 5 minutes, and form into two round loaves. Place them on a lightly greased baking sheet and leave them, covered, for another hour, or until well risen.

Preheat the oven to 400°F. Make an egg wash by beating the egg with the water. Brush the loaves with the wash, prick the tops with a fork, and bake for 15 minutes. Lower the heat to 350°F and continue baking for a further 30–35 minutes, or until the loaves sound hollow when tapped on the bottom. Cool the bread on wire racks and serve with unsalted butter.

BAKED POTATO AND APPLE PUREE

♦ ♦ ♦

PUDDING IZ KARTOPHELYA I YABLOK

In addition to potatoes, apples are another of Lithuania's passions, and they appear in everything from desserts to first courses with herring. This pudding also has variations in Denmark and Germany, where there is a predilection for sweet-spicy combinations. It goes particularly well with pork, goose and duck.

SERVES 4–6

- ◆ *1 lb floury potatoes, unpeeled*
- ◆ *1 lb tart apples, peeled*
- ◆ *¹/₂ cup butter*
- ◆ *2 tsp sugar*
- ◆ *¹/₄ tsp nutmeg*
- ◆ *³/₄ cup milk*
- ◆ *¹/₄ cup heavy cream*
- ◆ *6 tbsp fresh, or 4 tbsp dried breadcrumbs*

In a large saucepan, cover the potatoes with water and bring to the boil. Lower the heat and simmer until the potatoes are tender. Meanwhile, in another large saucepan, sauté the apples in ¹/₃ cup butter until softened. Toss the hot apples with the sugar and nutmeg, and set aside.

Drain the potatoes and peel while still hot. Mash them with the milk until as smooth as possible. Add the apples in their butter, and the cream. Mash and beat vigorously to combine.

Preheat the oven to 400°F. Transfer the mixture to a baking dish. Scatter the breadcrumbs over the top, and dot with the remaining butter. Bake for 25 minutes, or until the top is golden.

LITHUANIAN POTATO GRATIN

KUGELIS

◆ ◆ ◆

This is perhaps Lithuania's best-known dish. It is often served with a scattering of separately fried onions on top, but that does seem to be gilding the lily.

SERVES 4–6

- 2 lb baking potatoes, peeled and grated
- 1 tsp salt
- 2 small eggs
- 2 tbsp potato starch or plain flour
- ½ tsp baking powder
- 2 tbsp melted bacon fat
- 1 small onion, grated
- ½ tsp caraway seed crushed
- ¼ tsp pepper
- ¼ cup butter, melted

Toss the grated potatoes in a colander with the salt. Drain for 10 minutes then, with your hands, squeeze out as much liquid as possible and pat dry with absorbent paper towel.

Beat the eggs in a large bowl. Sift in the potato starch or flour and baking powder, and stir in the bacon fat, grated onion, caraway seed, and pepper. Add the potatoes and toss well to combine.

Preheat the oven to 350°F. Transfer the potatoes to a greased baking dish, smooth top, and pour the melted butter over. Bake the potatoes for 35 minutes, then increase the heat to 400°F and bake for a further 20 minutes, or until the top is golden brown. Serve immediately.

LATVIAN BURGERS WITH SOUR CREAM

KURZEMES

◆ ◆ ◆

This, together with *ligzdinas* – meatballs stuffed with hard-boiled eggs – is Latvia's best-known main course. Neither is a subtle dish, but they appeal to hearty appetites gained from working in the open air.

SERVES 6

- 2 tbsp vegetable oil
- 2 tbsp butter
- 2 onions, finely chopped
- ¼ lb mushrooms
- ½ lb finely chopped pork
- ½ lb finely chopped veal
- ¼ lb finely chopped ham
- 3 tbsp finely chopped fresh parsley
- ¼ tsp dried thyme
- salt and freshly ground black pepper
- 2 tbsp dry breadcrumbs
- 1 egg
- ¾ cup beef consommé or stock
- ⅔ cup sour cream

Melt half the oil and butter in a frying pan over medium heat. Add the onions, and sauté gently for about 6 minutes, or until they are just softened. With a slotted spoon, remove half the onions and set aside. Add the mushrooms to the pan, and continue cooking until they are very limp and most of the liquid has disappeared from the pan.

In a bowl, combine the three meats with the parsley, thyme, and salt and pepper to taste, and the mushrooms and onions from the pan. Use your hands to mix thoroughly, then add the breadcrumbs and egg, and continue to combine well. Shape the mixture into 6 patties and flatten them.

Add the remaining oil and butter to the pan. Melt over medium-high heat, and sauté the patties until the meat is browned on both sides, about 15 minutes. Pour over consommé or stock, together with the reserved onions, and cook over high heat until the liquid is reduced by half. Reduce the heat to low and remove the patties to a serving dish; keep warm. Stir the sour cream into the sauce and pour over the patties. Serve immediately.

ONION-AND-MUSTARD HERRINGS

SIPOLI MERCE

◆ ◆ ◆

Onions and mustard appear in combination with herring in several Baltic recipes; sometimes the fish is in the sauce, as in Lithuanian *silke cepts*. In this Latvian version, the marriage is a bit more subtle.

SERVES 4

- *1 1/2 lb fresh small herring, gutted, head, backbone and bones removed, washed and patted dry*
- *8 tbsp rye flour*
- *1/4 cup unsalted butter*
- *1 medium red onion, peeled, sliced and separated into rings*
- *2 tbsp finely chopped parsley*
- *lemon quarters*

For the coating

- *4 tbsp German-style mustard*
- *1 tbsp French-style mustard*
- *3 small egg yolks*
- *1/3 cup plus 1 tbsp heavy cream*
- *salt and freshly ground black pepper*

To make the coating mixture, mix together the two mustards in a small bowl. Whisk in the egg yolks, one by one, then the cream. Season to taste, and whisk again lightly.

Spread out one herring on a flat plate. Spoon a little of the coating over the inside of the fish, fold together, and brush the skin on both sides with the mixture. Push to one side of the plate and continue with each of the remaining fish. Use any remaining mixture to recoat the fish. Cover with foil, and leave overnight in the refrigerator.

Spread the rye flour on a plate, and dip each of the fish into it. Melt the butter in a large frying pan over medium heat. Fry the fish in batches, turning to cook both sides, until they are golden brown, about 6 minutes. Keep warm until all the fish are cooked.

Arrange the fish attractively on a serving dish, with the onion rings and parsley scattered over them. Serve garnished with lemon quarters.

BEETS WITH SWEET-SOUR DRESSING

SVYOKLA Z KISLO-SLADKOY PRIPRAVOY

◆ ◆ ◆

A Lithuanian treatment for beets. If the stalks and leaves are unavailable, use half the dressing on the beets and reserve the rest; it can be used to dress a celery and potato salad or carrot salad.

SERVES 6

- *2 lb small-to-medium fresh beets with attached stalks*

For the dressing

- *1 tsp dry mustard powder*
- *3 tbsp sugar*
- *1 1/2 tbsp honey*
- *1 tbsp fresh lemon juice*
- *1/2 cup white wine vinegar*
- *100 ml/ 4 fl oz white wine*
- *large pinch of paprika*
- *1 tsp caraway seeds*
- *1/2 cup vegetable oil*
- *2 tbsp finely chopped scallions*

To make the dressing, combine all the dressing ingredients except the oil and scallions in a bowl or blender. Whisk or process until combined, then add the oil in a steady stream, whisking (or running the motor) until the dressing is emulsified. Stir in the scallions and set aside.

Scrub the beets clean, and cut off the stalks and leaves leaving about 1 in from the top. Put the beets in a large stainless steel or enamelled saucepan, and cover with water. Place over high heat, cover and bring to the boil. Lower the heat, and simmer for about 15 minutes or until tender. Drain, allow to cool slightly, and slip off the skins.

Trim the stalks from the leafy green tops; wash and drain both separately. Chop the stalks into small pieces, place in another large saucepan, and add just enough water in which to steam them. Bring to the boil, cover, and simmer for about 5 minutes. Meanwhile, shred the greens; add them to the stalks and continue to cook until the green are wilted, about 3 minutes. Drain the greens thoroughly.

Cut off, and discard, the top ends of the beets and cut the beets into thin slices. In a bowl, toss in half the dressing. In another bowl, place the drained stalks and greens, and toss with the remainder of the dressing. Chill both in the refrigerator for at least 2 hours before serving.

Transfer to a serving dish with two compartments or, alternatively, arrange the greens in the center of a serving plate and surround with the sliced beets.

SALADS

HERRING, MEAT, AND BEET SALAD
ROSSOLYE

◆ ◆ ◆

Rossolye is a signature dish of Estonian cuisine, rather like *borsch* is of Russian. It is no surprise that both are based on beets. *Rossolye* is a common component of the Estonian version of the *zakuska* table, and makes a delicious luncheon dish on a warm summer's day.

SERVES 8

- *3 tsp dry mustard powder*
- *¹/₂ tsp sugar*
- *1¹/₄ cups whipping cream*
- *5 large boiled beets, peeled and diced*
- *2 tart apples, cored, peeled, and diced*
- *2 fillets of pickled herring, drained and diced*
- *1 lb leftover lean cooked beef or pork, trimmed and diced*
- *salt and freshly ground black pepper*
- *6 large potatoes, boiled, peeled and diced*
- *2 sweet-sour Polish-style chopped pickles, diced*
- *2–3 tbsp dry white wine*
- *2 hard-boiled eggs, chopped*
- *lettuce leaves*

To make the dressing, combine the mustard, sugar and whipping cream in a large bowl. By hand or with an electric mixer, whip the mustard cream until it holds soft peaks. Set aside.

In another large bowl, combine the beets, apples, potatoes, pickles, herrings, meat, seasoning to taste, and the wine. Toss to combine. Then gently fold in the hard-boiled eggs and three-quarters of the dressing. Chill for 30 minutes, then transfer the salad to a lettuce-lined plate or glass bowl and top with the remaining whipped cream.

CABBAGE PATTIES

KAPUSTNY RULET

◆ ◆ ◆

This recipe gives stuffed cabbage rolls, that well-loved East European dish, a distinct Estonian-Finnish twist, by burying the rolls under a layer of puffy yeast dough.

SERVES 6–8

- ◆ $1/2$ cup pearl barley
- ◆ 3 lb head white Dutch cabbage
- ◆ 2 tbsp vegetable oil
- ◆ 1 onion, finely chopped
- ◆ 1 small red sweet pepper, cored, seeded, and chopped
- ◆ $1/2$ lb finely chopped pork
- ◆ $1/2$ lb finely chopped veal
- ◆ 2 sweet-sour dill pickles, chopped
- ◆ $1^1/4$ cup chicken or beef stock
- ◆ salt and freshly ground black pepper
- ◆ 2 tbsp butter
- ◆ 4 tsp flour
- ◆ 1 tbsp tomato paste
- ◆ $2/3$ cup sour cream
- ◆ $1/2$ recipe sour-cream rye dough (page 77), or 1 lb packet wholewheat bread dough
- ◆ 1 large egg

Fill a large saucepan with water. Bring to the boil, add the barley, and lower the heat. Simmer, covered, until the barley is tender, about 30 minutes. Drain the barley thoroughly, and reserve.

Meanwhile, soften and remove the cabbage leaves as described on page 45. Repeat the process until you have about 18 leaves. Cut out the toughest part of the central stem in each leaf. Set aside.

Heat the oil in a frying pan, and stir in the onion. Sauté until limp, about 6 minutes. Add the pepper, and cook for another 5 minutes, until that, too, is limp. Take the mixture off the heat. Transfer to a bowl and add the meat, chopped pickles, 2 tbsp stock, and salt and pepper to taste. Use your hands to combine well, and divide into as many portions as there are leaves. Put a portion at the stalk end of each leaf, tuck in the ends, and roll to make a neat packet. Place the cabbage rolls in a baking dish just large enough to hold them in one layer. Set aside.

Melt the butter in a saucepan. Stir in the flour and cook for 3 minutes, or until the mixture is smooth. Whisk in the remaining stock and tomato paste; continue until the sauce boils and thickens. Take the sauce off the heat and stir in the sour cream. Pour the hot sauce evenly over the cabbage rolls.

Roll the dough out to a rectangle just larger than the baking dish. Lay over the top of the cabbage rolls and tuck the edges in. Use a fork to pull the dough gently towards the rim of the dish, crimping it. Cover the pastry with a dampened tea towel and leave to rise in a warm place for 20 minutes, or until risen and puffed up.

Preheat the oven to 350°F. Make an egg wash by lightly beating the egg with a little water. Brush the wash over the pastry and bake until golden brown, about 45 minutes.
45 minutes.

PORK LOIN WITH APPLE PRESERVES

SVINOYE FILYE Z KONSERVIROVANNYMI YABLOKAMI

◆ ◆ ◆

The accompanying preserve for this dish must be made at least 3 days ahead of time; the meat should be marinated for 24 hours. Leftover cooked meat, topped with the apple chutney, makes a particularly good cold sandwich on rye bread.

SERVES 4

- ◆ 2 lb rolled pork loin
- ◆ $1/2$ cup beer

For the marinade

- ◆ 1 tbsp honey
- ◆ 1 tbsp finely chopped fresh marjoram
- ◆ 1 tsp juniper berries, crushed
- ◆ 1 clove garlic, crushed
- ◆ $1/4$ tsp dried black peppercorns

For the preserve

- ◆ $1/3$ cup dry apple cider
- ◆ $3/4$ cup light brown sugar
- ◆ 3 dessert apples, peeled, cored, and chopped
- ◆ 1 small onion, finely chopped
- ◆ juice and rind of $1/2$ lemon
- ◆ $1/2$ red sweet pepper, cored, seeded, and chopped
- ◆ 1 clove garlic, crushed and finely chopped
- ◆ 2 tbsp finely chopped fresh peeled ginger
- ◆ large pinch cayenne pepper
- ◆ $1/4$ tsp salt

Make the preserve first. Bring the cider and brown sugar to the boil in a large saucepan; stir until the sugar dissolves. Add the remaining ingredients, and bring to the boil again. Reduce the heat and simmer, stirring occasionally, until the mixture is reduced to about $1^3/4$ cup. Cool, then chill for at least 3 days before using. (The preserve may be kept for up to 2 weeks in the refrigerator.)

Place the marinade ingredients in a large plastic bag. Add the pork loin and roll it around in the bag to coat it. Tie the bag shut and place on a dish in a cool place. Turn it occasionally in the next 24 hours.

Preheat the oven to 375°F. Decant the pork from the marinade and discard the marinade. Place the pork on a trivet over a baking tray, and roast until the meat is done, about 50-55 minutes. Remove the meat to a dish and keep warm.

Skim the fat from the drippings in the tray and discard. Pour the beer into the tray and bring the boil over high heat, stirring the dripping into the beer. Reduce the liquid until thickened. Pour into a sauceboat, and serve with the pork and preserves.

Pork Loin with Apple Preserves

POULTRY & MEAT

PICKLED AND COOKED GOOSE

GUS PRIGOTOVLYENNY V MARINADYE

◆ ◆ ◆

The cooking of Eastern Scandinavia has had a pronounced influence on the cuisine of Estonia. This recipe is a variation of an old Swedish dish; like ham, the cured goose could be kept until needed, a boon when refrigerators were unknown. The berry condiment is a typical Estonian touch.

SERVES 8

- ◆ *juice of ¹/₂ lemon*
- ◆ *²/₃ cup salt*
- ◆ *1¹/₂ tsp saltpeter*
- ◆ *10 lb goose, cleaned, washed, and dried*
- ◆ *¹/₂ lb canned lingonberries or cranberries, crushed*

For the brine and poaching broth

- ◆ *3 tbsp salt and 1 tbsp sugar to each 2¹/₂ cups water*
- ◆ *1 medium onion, unpeeled*
- ◆ *1 carrot, scraped*
- ◆ *1 clove garlic, unpeeled*
- ◆ *6 whole black peppercorns*
- ◆ *2 bay leaves*

Combine the lemon juice, salt, sugar and saltpeter in a bowl. Rub the goose all over inside and out with the mixture, being sure to reach all parts. Place in a shallow, non-metal baking dish or pan, and set aside in a cool place for 24 hours, turning it several times.

Place the goose in a large saucepan or pot. Add enough water to cover it and more, with about 1¹/₂ in to spare. Remove the goose and transfer the water with a measuring cup to a large bowl. Pour the water back into the pot and add salt and sugar in the proportions given in the ingredients list. Bring the brine to a rolling boil over high heat, then remove from the heat and leave to cool to room temperature.

When the brine is cool, put the goose into it. Weight the goose down to make sure it is totally submerged (a small weight inside the goose or a plate on top will do). Leave the bird in a cool place for 3 days, turning occasionally.

Lift out the goose and drain it thoroughly. Sew or skewer the openings shut and truss it. Place in a large saucepan or pot, and add just enough water to cover. Drop in the vegetables, garlic, peppercorns and bay leaves, and bring to the boil. Cover, lower the heat, and simmer gently for about 1³/₄ hours, or until the bird is fork-tender.

Drain the goose thoroughly and remove the trussing string and skewers. Serve warm or cold, with a sauceboat of the crushed lingonberries or cranberries on the side.

PASTRIES

SWEET CARAWAY BISCUITS

CEPUMI

◆ ◆ ◆

These sweet biscuits exhibit the Latvian love of caraway, even in sweet things.

MAKES ABOUT 48

- ◆ *¹/₂ cup unsalted butter, softened*
- ◆ *1 cup sugar*
- ◆ *1 egg*
- ◆ *2 tsp caraway seeds*
- ◆ *juice and grated rind of 1 small orange*
- ◆ *1³/₄ cup plain flour*
- ◆ *¹/₂ tsp baking soda*
- ◆ *¹/₄ tsp salt*

In a bowl, cream the butter with the sugar until light yellow and fluffy. Stir in the egg, caraway seeds, orange rind, and 2 tbsp of the juice. Combine thoroughly.

Sift the flour and salt into a bowl, and slowly stir into the butter mixture until you have a cohesive dough. Remove the dough from the bowl, and place on a 12 in long piece of waxed paper. Form the dough into a rough sausage and roll back and forth, wrapped in the paper, until the sausage is smooth and has become about 10 in long and 2 in wide. Wrap well in the paper and foil, and freeze until solid. Preheat the oven to 350°F. Cut the sausage into ¹/₄ in slices, and bake for 10–12 minutes, until the edges are golden brown.

Sweet Caraway Biscuits

SWEET APPLE BREAD PUDDING WITH LEMON SAUCE

SLADKY PUDDING Z YABLOKAMI I LIMONNOY PODLIVKOY

◆ ◆ ◆

The valued apple makes another appearance in this Lithuanian dessert, the sugar addict's answer to the savory Potato and Apple Pudding on page 60. Vanilla ice cream makes a delicious cold partner for this warm pudding, as do mashed and sugared cranberries.

SERVES 6–8

- ◆ $^1/_2$ cup unsalted butter
- ◆ $1^3/_4$ cups milk
- ◆ $^1/_2$ cup light brown sugar
- ◆ 6 slices stale white bread, crusts removed, cubed
- ◆ 2 dessert apples, peeled, cored, and sliced
- ◆ 2 eggs

- ◆ $^1/_4$ cup Greek- or Bulgarian-style yogurt
- ◆ $^1/_2$ tsp vanilla essence
- ◆ dash of almond essence
- ◆ $^1/_4$ tsp ground allspice
- ◆ $^1/_4$ tsp salt
- ◆ $^1/_2$ - $^2/_3$ cup dates, stoned and finely chopped
- ◆ 5 tsp wheatgerm

For the sauce

- ◆ $^3/_4$ cup sugar
- ◆ 2 tbsp cornstarch
- ◆ $1^1/_4$ cups water

- ◆ 3 tbsp butter
- ◆ 3 tbsp fresh lemon juice

Heat the butter, milk, and sugar together in a saucepan over low heat until the butter has melted and the sugar has dissolved. Set aside.

Combine the bread cubes and apple slices in a baking pan that will take them in one layer. In a bowl, whisk together the eggs, yogurt, vanilla and almond essences, the allspice and salt. Stir in the milk mixture and the dates.

Pour the liquid over the apples and bread, and leave to soak for 10–15 minutes. Meanwhile, preheat the oven to 350°F. Sprinkle the top of the pudding with the wheatgerm and bake for 40 minutes, or until puffy and golden brown.

Meanwhile, make the sauce. In a saucepan, stir the sugar and cornstarch in the water over high heat until boiling. Add the butter and lemon juice, stirring, and when the butter is dissolved, remove from the heat.

Serve the apple bread pudding warm, accompanied by the warm lemon sauce.

BIG BERRY DESSERT PANCAKES
PANNKOOGID

◆ ◆ ◆

These Estonian pancakes are huge – the size of plates – and have a fluffy consistency quite unlike the familiar pancake. In their native surroundings they would often be served with lingonberries – but raspberries or blueberries are just as scrumptious.

SERVES 6

- ◆ *1 cup plain flour*
- ◆ *2 tbsp sugar*
- ◆ *pinch of salt*

- ◆ *2 eggs, separated*
- ◆ *1 cup milk*
- ◆ *¹/₂ tsp vanilla essence*

For the filling

- ◆ *¹/₂ lb fresh raspberries or blueberries*
- ◆ *2 tbsp water*

- ◆ *¹/₂ cup sugar*
- ◆ *1 tbsp cornstarch*

Sift the flour, sugar, and salt into a large bowl. Make a well in the center. Drop the egg yolks, the milk and vanilla into the well, then beat to combine thoroughly with the flour. The batter will be thin. Cover it with a cloth and leave in a cool – not cold – place overnight to mature.

To make the filling, rinse and drain the berries and place in an enamelled or stainless steel saucepan, together with the water and the sugar. Cook over medium-high heat, stirring, until the berries begin dissolving into a sauce, with some remaining whole. Bring to the boil, stir in the cornstarch and reduce the heat. Cook for 5–10 minutes, stirring until the filling mixture has thickened. Remove from the heat, pour into an attractive bowl, and allow to cool.

Before using the batter, beat the egg whites in a large bowl until they form stiff peaks. With a rubber or plastic spatula, carefully fold them into the batter.

Lightly coat a large, non-stick crêpe or frying pan with butter, and heat until medium-hot. Remove from the heat and pour in ¹/₂ cup of the batter. Tilt the pan to spread it evenly, then replace on the heat and fry the pancake for about 3 minutes on each side, until golden brown. Slide the pancake onto a dish and keep warm while you make the rest of the pancakes.

Serve each pancake flat on a plate, accompanied by the bowl of fruit sauce.

FROM FARMLAND AND BREADBASKET
Ukraine, Belorussia, and Moldova

ALL THREE EASTERN STATES OF THE CIS SHARE
A COMMON LEGACY OF "BORDERDOM," BUT EACH HAS
RESPONDED TO ITS SITUATION IN A DIFFERENT WAY.
BELORUSSIA AND MOLDOVA EXHIBIT PERHAPS STRONGER
CHARACTERISTICS OF THEIR GENEALOGICAL "DISTAFF"
SIDES – POLAND AND ROMANIA, RESPECTIVELY –
BUT THEY HAVE SHOWN THEMSELVES LESS VOLATILE
POLITICALLY AND LESS NATIONALISTIC THAN
THE UKRAINIAN GIANT.

Though a separate republic with a people fiercely proud of their different language, literature, culture and cuisine, the Ukraine is, in fact, the cradle of Russian civilization. Kiev, its capital, was originally the premier town and capital of Russ, the first unified "Russian-Slavic" state, founded in the 9th century. At its height, the kingdom stretched from the Baltic to the Volga and Danube; its rulers crushed invaders from the south and east, and assimilated its previous Scandinavian lords. However, by the 12th and 13th centuries, disputes over successions, devastating attacks by the Tartars and the expansion of the Polish-Lithuanian alliance had pushed the center of power to the east – to Novgorod, and eventually, to Moscow.

The early importance of Kiev-Rus is echoed in the influence of Ukrainian food. The ubiquitous beet was an introduction to Russia from the Ukraine, as was *borsch* itself. Here even the green tops of the beet are treated with respect. Peter the Great's present to his people, the potato, was exploited to the fullest in the fields and kitchens of the Ukraine and Belorussia, to make its circuitous way back into the repertoire of heartland Russia. There is good reason, too, why the Ukraine was known as the "breadbasket" of the old Union; both fields of grain and traditional creativity in baking have resulted in a fabled

70 types of loaves, rolls and buns, ranging from white to black, plain or studded with caraway or poppy seeds, and flavored with rye, sour cream, honey, or molasses.

Within the old Soviet Union, the Ukrainians have always carried a reputation as chefs, using a greater variety both of ingredients and cooking methods than the Russians. Because the Ukraine stretches into the Crimea, historical home to immigrant Tartars and Turks as well as Slavs, eastern influences permeated northwards. From these regions came the Eastern and Middle-Eastern taste for honey, nuts, citrus and dried fruits in both sweet and spicy dishes.

The cooking of the smaller republics of Belorussia and Moldova exhibit notably more "non-Russian" tendencies than that of their huge sprawling neighbor to the north. The borders of the former have moved east and west between Russia and Poland for centuries, and the food of the region displays that dichotomy. Pigs have overtaken cattle in agricultural and culinary importance, while Eastern Polish specialties like crispy pork fat in dripping (used as a spread for bread), a wide variety of ham sausages, *zrazy* (beef rolls stuffed with sour pickles, eggs and/or vegetables), Polish-style *golubtsy* (without tomatoes or sour cream), the preference of sauerkraut to fresh cabbage, and a weakness for poppyseed pastries became Belorussian fixtures. As in urban Poland, the cuisines of Minsk and Brest show the influence of the huge Jewish communities that once flourished there.

Moldova, to all intents and purposes, is an outpost of Romania. Its stews and sausages can be surprisingly spicy; red and navy beans, corn, fresh peppers, grilled meats, and fresh, smoked and aged ewe's cheeses speak more of the Balkans and the Levant than of northern steppes. Here, too, begins the wine belt that extends into the Crimea and on to Georgia; its vineyards boast more than 100 varieties of red, white, rosé, and champagne wines. Unfamiliar with modern technological developments in oenology, their labels unknown in the west, they promise a bonanza for future generations of wine lovers once the new openness in communications allows progress to make its way in this time-locked region.

◁ *Lvov, in the Ukraine, was the scene of violent nationalist demonstrations in October 1989. In more peaceful times, the gilded,* **fin-de-siècle** *opera theater* (center) *is a focus for the city's cultural activity.*

In Kishinev, capital of Moldova, a guard of honour patrols the monument to soldiers killed in the Second World War.

"ALMOST NOTHING" SOUP

POCHTY NICHEVO

◆ ◆ ◆

This soup, made from scraps, has a surprising flavor, smoky and nut-like. Add a little cream, to make it more sophisticated.

SERVES 4 – 6

- ◆ *3 lb beef, chicken, veal or mixed bones*
- ◆ *1 onion, unpeeled*
- ◆ *salt and freshly ground black pepper*
- ◆ *8¼ cups water*
- ◆ *2 lb potatoes, scrubbed and dried*
- ◆ *½ cup bacon fat or melted butter*
- ◆ *1 large onion, peeled and chopped*
- ◆ *½ cup light cream (optional)*
- ◆ *2 tbsp chopped fresh chives*

Place the bones, the unpeeled onion, and seasoning to taste in a large pot. Cover with the water, and put over high heat. Bring to the boil, then cover and simmer for 1 hour. Uncover and continue to simmer until the stock has reduced by almost half. Strain the stock and return to the saucepan.

Meanwhile peel the potatoes. Reserve the potatoes themselves for another use. Melt the bacon fat or butter in a frying pan and sauté the onion until soft, about 6 minutes. Add the potato skins and continue to cook until they too are tender.

Transfer the potato skins and onion to the saucepan containing the stock. Bring to the boil, then reduce the heat and simmer for 10 minutes. Purée the soup in batches; return to the saucepan and reheat. Thin, if necessary, with a little water or the cream. Ladle into individual bowls and serve sprinkled with the chopped chives.

BLACK BREAD SOUP

ZUPA KHLEBOVA

◆ ◆ ◆

This is another soup born of poverty and bad harvests –
yet it is filling and extremely flavorful. It is a meal in itself
rather than a delicate preliminary to an elegant repast,
and can be accompanied by warm *pierogi* and followed by
salad. Ukrainian croutons are traditionally fried in pork
dripping or bacon fat.

SERVES 6

◆ *1 large carrot, halved and sliced*
◆ *1 large leek, sliced*
◆ *1 celery stick, sliced*
◆ *2 onions, chopped*
◆ *1 parsnip, chopped*
◆ *generous ³/₄ cup lima beans*
◆ *5³/₄ cups beef stock*
◆ *2¹/₄ cups stale black bread, cubed*

◆ *salt and freshly ground black pepper*
◆ *150 ml/¹/₄ pt buttermilk*
◆ *¹/₂ cup milk*
◆ *2 large egg yolks, lightly beaten*
◆ *fried croutons*
◆ *large pinch of nutmeg*

Place all the vegetables in a large saucepan. Add the beef stock
and bring to a boil over high heat. Add the bread, reduce the
heat, cover, and simmer for about 40 minutes or until all the
vegetables are tender.

Purée the soup in batches in a blender or food processor
until as smooth as possible; return to the saucepan. Add
seasoning to taste and stir in the buttermilk and milk. Heat
until simmering, but do not boil.

Spoon a small amount of the hot soup into the beaten eggs,
then quickly stir the eggs into the soup in the saucepan.
Remove from the heat immediately, and pour the soup into a
tureen. Scatter fried croutons over the top and a sprinkling of
nutmeg; offer more croutons in a separate bowl.

MOLDOVAN POTATO-CHEESE SOUP

MOLDAVSKY SUP IZ SYRA I KARTOPHELYA

◆ ◆ ◆

This is a soup for potato-lovers, traditionally made with
aged *brynza*, a hard ewe's cheese. It is lip-smacking good
made with the Basque variety. You can use cheddar instead
of ewe's cheese, but the results will not be as authentic.

SERVES 6

◆ *¹/₄ cup unsalted butter*
◆ *2 large onions, finely chopped*
◆ *3 large carrots, chopped*
◆ *2 large potatoes, peeled and chopped*
◆ *¹/₄ tsp sweet paprika*
◆ *large pinch of cayenne pepper*

◆ *1 tbsp finely chopped parsley*
◆ *5 cups chicken stock*
◆ *¹/₂ lb ewe's cheese or cheddar*
◆ *salt and freshly ground black pepper*
◆ *finely snipped chives*

Melt the butter in a large saucepan over medium heat.
Add the onions and carrots and sauté gently for about 20–25
minutes, until they are tender and lightly colored.

Stir in the potatoes, spices and parsley, then add the
chicken stock and bring to the boil. Reduce the heat, cover,
and simmer for 30 minutes, or until the potatoes are soft.

Strain the soup into a bowl, and purée the vegetables in a
blender or food processor with a little of the stock until
smooth. Return the purée to the saucepan and add as much
stock as necessary (about 4¹/₄ cups) to obtain a good
consistency. Set the soup over low heat and stir in the cheese.

Continue stirring until it has dissolved into the soup, but do
not allow to boil. Adjust the seasoning to taste and serve
immediately in individual bowls, topped with the snipped
chives.

BREADS

GRILLED CORNMEAL CAKE WITH CHEESE

MAMALYGA

◆ ◆ ◆

Moldovan food exhibits a legacy of the days between the wars when it was a part of Romania, and of the generations before that when it had many unofficial links with that country. This polenta-like hard cake has a Balkan flavor; it is often served with *borsch* or cabbage dishes.

SERVES 6

- ◆ *²/₃ cup stone-ground yellow cornmeal*
- ◆ *4¹/₄ cups water*
- ◆ *1–1¹/₂ tsp salt*
- ◆ *¹/₄ cup butter*
- ◆ *pinch of dried marjoram*

- ◆ *large pinch of cayenne pepper*
- ◆ *10 oz hard ewe's or goat's cheese*
- ◆ *salt and freshly ground black pepper*

Stir the cornmeal in a large frying pan over medium heat for 4 minutes, or until it loses its bright yellow color and becomes light beige.

Pour the water into a saucepan. Put the hot cornmeal into the water (it should hiss); then stir in the salt to taste. Cook over moderate heat for 5 minutes, stirring, until the liquid begins to boil. Cover, lower the heat and simmer for 20 minutes, stirring frequently.

Preheat the oven to 375°F. Uncover the saucepan and continue to stir until the polenta is very thick and the spoon is drawing it away from the bottom and sides of the pan. Remove from the heat, add the butter, marjoram and pepper, and stir until the butter is melted into the polenta. Stir in three-quarters of the cheese, then turn the polenta into a shallow buttered baking dish.

Bake for 40 minutes on the top shelf of the oven, until the cake has a skin over it. Remove from the oven and allow to cool and set for at least 1 hour. (The cake can be kept refrigerated for up to 3 days.)

To serve, heat the broiler. Slice the cake into squares or wedges and sprinkle over the remaining cheese. Broil until the cheesy crust is golden-brown and the *mamalyga* is hot. Serve immediately.

SOUR CREAM RYE ROLLS

BALABUSKY

◆ ◆ ◆

The Ukraine is renowned for the variety of its breads. These rolls are one of the types most commonly encountered. They make delicious sandwiches when filled with smoked ham, kolbasa or salt beef, spread with plenty of mustard.

MAKES 10–12 ROLLS

- $^3/_4$ cup lukewarm water
- $2^1/_2$ tsp (1 x $^1/_4$ oz packet) active dry yeast
- 1 tbsp sugar
- $^1/_2$ cup sour cream
- 1 cup rye flour
- 2–$2^1/_2$ cups plain flour
- $1^1/_2$–2 tsp salt
- $1^1/_2$ tbsp caraway seeds

Place the water in a large bowl and sprinkle the yeast and sugar into it. Leave for 5–8 minutes, or until the mixture is foamy. Stir in the sour cream, then slowly work in the rye flour and 2 cups of the plain flour. Add salt to taste and 1 tbsp of the caraway seeds. Work the dough with your hands until it forms a ball, and turn out onto a floured surface. Knead in as much of the remaining flour as will make the dough smooth and still slightly sticky; this will take about 8–10 minutes.

Transfer the dough to a buttered bowl, turning it to coat with butter, then cover the bowl with plastic wrap and leave to rise in a warm place for 1 hour or until doubled in volume. Turn the dough out onto a floured surface, and pull into 10–12 equal pieces. Shape each into a flat-bottomed oval, then

scatter the remaining caraway seeds over the tops and press in lightly.

Place the ovals on a lightly-oiled baking tray and leave to rise, covered with a damp tea towel, for 45–60 minutes, or until doubled in size.

Preheat the oven to 400°F. Bake the rolls for 18–20 minutes, or until they are golden brown. (The rolls may be frozen. Reheat wrapped in foil for 30 minutes at 375°F.)

EGG NOODLES AND BUCKWHEAT GROATS

LOKSHYNA Z KASHA

◆ ◆ ◆

Noodles and dumplings of all types are popular in the Ukraine and Belorussia. They range from little misshapen egg pasta droplets to potato and rice dumplings. They are served on their own with butter, accompanied by meat sauces, or baked with other ingredients, as here.

SERVES 6–8

- $^1/_2$ cup unsalted butter
- 2 onions, sliced
- $^1/_2$ lb field or brown mushrooms, sliced
- 6 oz whole buckwheat groats (kasha)
- 1 large egg, beaten
- $1^3/_4$ cup boiling water
- 1 tsp salt
- $^1/_2$ lb fresh egg noodles, cut into quarters
- freshly ground black pepper
- 8 tbsp fine dry breadcrumbs
- sour cream

Melt 2 tbsp butter in a large frying pan, and sauté the onions until they are soft and lightly coloured, about 8 minutes. Add the mushrooms and cook, stirring, until the mushrooms are soft. Transfer the vegetables to a casserole.

Wash and dry the frying pan. Place over moderate heat and add the buckwheat, stirring, and the beaten egg. Continue to stir until the groats are separate and egg-coated. Pour in the boiling water and add 1 tbsp butter and the salt. Cover and simmer until all the liquid is absorbed and the buckwheat just tender, about 25 minutes. Transfer the buckwheat to the casserole.

Preheat the oven to 350°F. In a large saucepan, cook the noodles in boiling water until just tender, about 4 minutes. Drain thoroughly and stir the noodles into the casserole with the buckwheat, onions and mushrooms, adding 3 tbsp butter and seasoning to taste. Melt the remaining butter and combine with the breadcrumbs. Scatter over the top of the casserole, and bake in the oven until warmed through and the breadcrumbs are toasted, about 20 minutes. Serve with a sauceboat of sour cream.

MINSK-STYLE EGGS

JAJKA MINSKY

◆ ◆ ◆

These eggs make a frequent appearance at Christmas and Easter festivities. They are traditionally eaten warm, with horn spoons, but they are also good cold.

SERVES 8

- 10 hard-boiled eggs
- ⅓ cup unsalted butter, softened
- 1 tbsp mayonnaise
- 2 tbsp heavy cream
- 3½ tbsp fresh dill
- 2 tsp sweet paprika
- 1 tbsp finely chopped fresh parsley
- 4 tbsp dry breadcrumbs
- 3 tbsp grated Gruyère cheese
- 16 anchovy fillets, rinsed, dried, and cut in half lengthways
- fresh watercress sprigs

Halve the eggs and carefully remove the yolks. Set aside the 16 best whites.

In a bowl, mash the yolks well with the softened butter. Beat in the mayonnaise, heavy cream, dill, paprika, parsley, and seasoning to taste. Finely chop the 4 extra whites and stir them into the mixture. Divide the filling between the 16 reserved egg whites.

Preheat the oven to 400°F. Place the filled eggs on a baking tray. Mix together the breadcrumbs and grated cheese, and sprinkle evenly over the yolks. Cross each egg with two strips of anchovy to make an "X." Bake for 10 minutes, until the eggs are warmed through and the tops are golden.

Arrange sprigs of watercress on 8 plates, and put 2 egg-halves on each plate. Serve warm.

ODESSA-STYLE MUSHROOMS IN SOUR CREAM

ZULYNEZ GRIBNOY PO-ODESSKY

◆ ◆ ◆

The combination of mushrooms and sour cream is a popular one all over the Ukraine, Belorussia and Moldova, and understandably, as it is mouthwateringly delicious. However, the version that originates from the holiday port of Odessa, on the Black Sea, has a widespread reputation among cognoscenti. At home it would be made with *brynza* or *seerh*, but Monterey Jack cheese makes a good substitute.

SERVES 6

- ⅓ cup plus 1 tbsp unsalted butter, at room temperature
- 4 scallions, finely chopped
- 1 lb field or brown mushrooms, wiped and patted dry
- 1 tbsp flour
- salt and freshly ground black pepper
- ½ cup sour cream
- ⅓ cup plus 1 tbsp heavy cream
- 2 oz Monterey Jack, grated

Melt ¼ cup of the butter in a frying pan over medium heat. Add the scallions and sauté briefly, then stir in the mushrooms and continue to cook for about 5–6 minutes, until the mushrooms are browned and just going soft.

In a small bowl, combine 1 tbsp butter with the flour, working it to make a smooth consistency. Stir the mixture into the mushrooms and cook for 3 minutes, or until thickened. Season to taste, and stir in the sour cream and heavy cream.

Preheat the oven to 350°F. Pour the mushroom mixture into an attractive baking dish. Sprinkle the top with the cheese, and dot with the remaining butter. Bake for 20–25 minutes, until the mushrooms are bubbling and the top just coloring.

Odessa Style Mushrooms in Sour Cream

PICKLED WATERMELON RIND

MARINOVANNYA ARBUZNAYA KORKA

◆ ◆ ◆

**Pickled watermelon rind is a common addition to a *zakuska*
table, its sweet-sour tang a perfect complement to meat- and
cheese-based dishes.**

MAKES ABOUT 2 QUARTS

- ◆ *2 lb watermelon rind*
- ◆ *¹/₃ cup salt*
- ◆ *11¹/₄ cups water*
- ◆ *2¹/₂ cups cider vinegar*
- ◆ *1 tsp whole cloves*
- ◆ *1 cinnamon stick*
- ◆ *2 slices root ginger, peeled
  and crushed*
- ◆ *1 tsp whole allspice*
- ◆ *4 cups sugar*

Pare the rind carefully of any pink flesh, and remove the thin
green peel on the surface. Cut into 1 x ¹/₂ in pieces. Place
them in a bowl with the salt and 10 cups water to cover. Leave
overnight.

Drain the rind, rinse thoroughly with cold water, and drain
again. Put the rind in a large enamelled or stainless steel
saucepan with 1¹/₄ cup water and the vinegar. Cover and boil
the rind, stirring occasionally, until it is softened. Tie the
spices in a cheesecloth bag and drop into the pot; stir in the
sugar until it is dissolved. Bring the mixture to the boil, and
cook over high heat until the rind is transparent.

Transfer the rind to sterilized Mason jars. Reduce the syrup
a further 5 minutes, then pour over the rinds and seal the jars.
Allow to cool, then keep in a cold dark place until needed.

CABBAGE SOUFFLÉ

NAKYPLIAK

◆ ◆ ◆

***Nakypliak* is considered the test of a good Ukrainian cook.
Following traditional methods of preparation and steaming,
it takes several days and much work to prepare, but this
version cuts a few corners – it still requires time, but the
workload has been lightened. The result is still a revelation.**

SERVES 4

- ◆ *¹/₂ a small white cabbage
  (about ³/₄ lb), outer leaves
  removed, cored and cut
  into three wedges*
- ◆ *salt and freshly ground
  black pepper*
- ◆ *large pinch of sweet paprika*
- ◆ *¹/₄ tsp caraway seeds*
- ◆ *¹/₃ cup bacon fat or butter*
- ◆ *1 onion, finely chopped*
- ◆ *1 clove garlic, crushed*
- ◆ *3 tbsp flour*
- ◆ *large pinch of cayenne
  pepper*
- ◆ *³/₄ cup plus 2 tbsp milk*
- ◆ *5 oz Gruyère cheese,
  grated*
- ◆ *3 eggs separated*
- ◆ *2 tbsp breadcrumbs mixed
  with a little melted butter*

Shred the cabbage wedges as thinly as possible, and place in a
large bowl with a wide mouth. Sprinkle 2 tsp salt over the
cabbage. Toss, and squeeze the salt into the cabbage to soften
it. Place a plate on top of the cabbage, and a small weight on
the plate. Place a tea towel over the top of the bowl. Leave for
several hours in a warm place (a sunny windowsill for
example), until the cabbage is juicy. Then pour boiling water
over the cabbage so that the plate is just submerged, and tie
the tea towel over the bowl. Leave the bowl in a warm place
for 3–4 days before continuing with the recipe.

When ready to proceed, drain the cabbage. Rinse it
thoroughly in cold water, then drain well again. Place the
cabbage in a saucepan, add a little boiling water and the
caraway seeds, and cook over low heat, uncovered, for about
20 minutes, stirring occasionally until the cabbage is soft and
the water evaporated. Drain the cabbage in a colander,
pressing with a spoon to make sure that as much liquid as
possible has been removed. Allow the cabbage to cool to room
temperature.

Meanwhile, melt the bacon fat or butter in a flameproof
casserole and sauté the onion until soft and lightly
colored, about 6 minutes. Add the garlic and cook for another
2 minutes, then stir in the flour and cook for a further 2
minutes. Take off the heat and stir in the cayenne pepper,
paprika and seasoning to taste and, little by little, the milk.
Return to the heat and bring to the boil, stirring until it
begins to thicken. Remove from the heat again and beat in the
cheese, followed by the egg yolks.

Preheat the oven to 375°F. Stir the cooled cabbage into the
sauce. In a bowl, whisk the egg whites until stiff but not dry.
Fold them lightly into the cabbage mixture. Spoon the
mixture into a greased soufflé dish and scatter the
breadcrumbs over the top. Bake in the oven for 40 minutes
until risen, lightly browned and set. Serve at once, while the
soufflé is piping hot.

CHICKEN KIEV
KOTLETY PO-KIEVSKY

• • •

Chicken Kiev has become a familiar dish, stacked frozen and ready-to-heat in supermarkets and frequently appearing on menus. But the real thing bears little resemblance, in appearance or taste, to such orange monstrosities. The recipe has been simplified to take advantage of prepared chicken breasts.

SERVES 6

- $^3/_4$ cup unsalted butter, softened
- grated rind and juice of 1 large lemon
- 3 tbsp freshly chopped tarragon
- 6 large skinless chicken breast fillets
- salt and freshly ground black pepper
- 2 small eggs
- $2^1/_3$ cups fresh fine breadcrumbs
- oil for deep-frying

Combine the butter, lemon rind, and tarragon in a bowl. With a fork, work the mixture until it is thoroughly mixed. Shape into a block, wrap in foil, and chill until hard.

Lay the chicken breasts on a sheet of waxed paper. Trim away any bits attached by membrane. Cover the breasts with another sheet of waxed paper and pound with a mallet until they are flattened. Season the fillets as desired.

Cut the butter block into 6 pieces, and place one piece in the center of each fillet. Fold the top and edges over, then roll neatly. Tie the roll with thread.

Beat the eggs lightly in a shallow bowl. Spread the breadcrumbs on a large plate. Dip the breast rolls in the egg then coat them in the breadcrumbs, pressing into the crumbs to make sure they adhere. To obtain a thick "skin" brush the coated rolls with a little more egg, if necessary, and press into the crumbs again. Place the rolls on a plate and chill for 2–3 hours.

In a deep fryer or heavy saucepan, heat enough oil to cover the breasts completely. When it spits at water droplets (or reaches 375°F), lower in 3 breasts with a slotted spoon. Fry until golden-brown, about 5–6 minutes. (The oil must not get too hot or the coating will brown before the chicken is cooked.) Drain on paper towels, and repeat with the remaining 3 breasts. Serve immediately. Potatoes and cabbage or peas would make a typical accompaniment.

STEWED LAMB WITH MUSHROOMS AND BARLEY

TYSHYONAYA BARANINAZ GRIBAMI I YACHMENYOM

◆ ◆ ◆

This is a Moldovan dish, from the foothills of the Carpathian mountains. It is unsophisticated and hardly pretty-pretty, but it is nutritious, inexpensive and full-flavored, a true rustic feast.

SERVES 6

- ◆ 2$\frac{1}{2}$ lb shanks or neck of lamb, cut into pieces
- ◆ scant $\frac{1}{2}$ cup vegetable oil
- ◆ 1 medium onion, chopped
- ◆ 2 long, red, medium-hot peppers, seeded and chopped
- ◆ 6 oz field or button mushrooms, wiped and sliced
- ◆ 1 tbsp German-style mustard
- ◆ 3$\frac{1}{4}$ cups chicken stock

- ◆ $\frac{1}{3}$ cup plus 1 tbsp white wine vinegar
- ◆ 1 cup pearl barley
- ◆ 1 tsp cumin seeds
- ◆ 2 whole cloves
- ◆ 2 tsp dried dill
- ◆ salt and freshly ground black pepper
- ◆ 1 cup sour cream or yogurt
- ◆ handful parsley, finely chopped

In a heavy casserole, brown the lamb shank or neck pieces in half the oil, until they are colored. Remove with a slotted spoon and set aside. Add the onion to the casserole, and cook until it is soft and lightly colored, about 6–8 minutes. Remove

with the slotted spoon and set aside. Add the rest of the oil, and sauté the red peppers and mushroom for about 5 minutes, or until the mushrooms are softened. Remove to a bowl and set aside.

Preheat the oven to 325°F. Stir the onions and lamb back into the casserole, together with the mustard. Add the chicken stock and the wine vinegar, bring to the boil, and transfer the casserole to the oven. Bake for 1$\frac{1}{2}$ hours, until the lamb is very tender and falling off the bones.

Remove the lamb from the casserole. Using your hands and a fork, pull the meat from the bones and chop it. Return to the casserole and stir into the stock with the barley, cumin seeds, cloves, dill, and seasoning to taste. Bring to the boil, cover, and lower the heat. Simmer for about 1 hour, until the barley is tender and most of the stock has been absorbed.

Stir the red pepper and mushrooms into the stew, together with the sour cream or yogurt. Heat through for about 10–12 minutes, take off the heat, stir in the chopped parsley, and bring to the table to serve.

SPICED OXTAILS WITH BUCKWHEAT

BYCHYI KHVOSTY Z KASHEY

◆ ◆ ◆

In the Russian and Polish countryside you can still see oxen pulling ploughs, and rough-looking horses trotting in front of wooden carts. A tough, gelatinous meat, oxtail needs slow cooking but the resulting tender flesh, falling off the bone, and the rich, thick sauce are worth the wait. This recipe is an adaptation from the Lower Volga region, nearing the Caspian Sea.

SERVES 6–8

- 5 lb oxtail pieces, trimmed
- 1/3 cup plus 1 tbsp sunflower oil
- 3 medium onions, sliced
- 4 cloves garlic, crushed
- 1 1/2 tbsp tomato paste
- 14 oz can chopped chilli tomatoes
- 3 3/4 cups beef stock
- 3 cinnamon sticks
- 1 tsp ground cumin
- 1 tsp ground ginger
- 1 tsp mustard seeds
- 3/4 tsp turmeric
- 4 tbsp finely chopped parsley
- 4 tbsp finely chopped coriander (cilantro)

- 3/4 lb coarse buckwheat groats
- 2 1/2 cups boiling water
- salt and freshly ground black pepper
- 1 tbsp butter
- 3 carrots, halved and thinly sliced
- 3/4 lb turnips, halved and thinly sliced
- 1 small celeriac, quartered and thinly sliced
- 2 medium zucchini, halved and thinly sliced
- 1/2 lb baby leeks, trimmed and left whole
- parsley and/or coriander sprigs, to garnish

In a large enamelled or stainless steel casserole, brown the oxtails in the oil. Remove with a slotted spoon to a plate and set aside. Add the onion to the pot and fry gently over medium heat until lightly colored and soft. Stir in the garlic and cook for 1 minute, then stir in the tomato paste, the tomatoes and their juice, and the beef stock. Drop in the cinnamon sticks, and stir in the cumin, ginger, mustard seeds, turmeric, parsley, and coriander. Bring to the boil, then cover and lower the heat. Simmer for 4 hours over a low heat, until the meat from the larger pieces is falling off the bone. If necessary, add water to keep the stock covering the meat.

Take the casserole off the heat and allow to cool. Refrigerate for 12 hours or overnight .

Preheat the oven to 350°F. Dry roast the buckwheat in a frying pan over medium-high heat, stirring constantly, until it begins to pop. Add the boiling water and salt to taste. Dot the butter over the surface and bake in the oven for 45 minutes, or until the grains are soft. Keep warm.

Meanwhile, lift off the solidified fat from the top of the casserole. With a slotted spoon, take out the oxtails, place them in a large baking dish, and pour over enough boiling water to cover the bottom of the dish to about 1/2 in. Cover the dish with foil, and reheat in the oven for the last 30 minutes while the buckwheat is cooking.

Strain the stock from the casserole into a bowl and discard the solids. Return the stock to the casserole and add the carrots, turnips, and celeriac. Bring to the boil, then cover and simmer the vegetables for 15 minutes, or until they are tender-crisp. Stir in the zucchini slices and the baby leeks, and cook for a further 5–10 minutes until they are also soft.

Drain the sauce through a strainer into a saucepan. Set the vegetables aside. Strain the reheated oxtails, allowing the cooking liquid to flow into the same saucepan. Quickly bring the sauce to a boil.

Pile the cooked buckwheat onto a large serving dish. Spoon the strained vegetables on top of the buckwheat, and surround it with the oxtails. Drizzle some of the sauce over the vegetables and buckwheat, and serve the remainder separately in a sauceboat. Garnish the dish with the sprigs of parsley and/or coriander.

FISH

NEMAN RIVER CARP IN KVAS AND LEMON

NEMANSKY KARP V KVASYE

◆ ◆ ◆

Though a staple of the Western Russian, Polish and Jewish diet, carp has not found much favor on the American table, largely because its bones make it a difficult fish to eat. This dish overcomes the problem, however, by boning the carp and cutting it into strips.

SERVES 6

- ◆ 4–5 lb carp, cleaned, head and backbone removed
- ◆ salt and freshly ground black pepper
- ◆ 3 tbsp unsalted butter
- ◆ 8 scallions, finely chopped
- ◆ 2 tsp brown sugar
- ◆ 1/2 bay leaf
- ◆ 5 juniper berries, crushed
- ◆ grated rind and juice of 1 small lemon
- ◆ 1 3/4 cups kvas or flat beer
- ◆ 3 tbsp crushed ginger biscuits
- ◆ handful flat-leaved parsley, finely chopped

Wash and dry the fish thoroughly. Cut into 1 1/2 in wide strips and sprinkle with salt. Chill for 1 hour.

In a heavy enamelled or stainless-steel casserole, melt the butter over medium heat and sauté the onions for 2 minutes, stirring. Add the sugar, herbs, lemon juice and rind, and pepper to taste. Stir for a couple of minutes to combine, then pour in the *kvas* and simmer for 20 minutes.

Strain into a bowl, discard the solids, then return the stock to the saucepan. Stir in the crushed ginger biscuits, and cook until they have dissolved into a mush. Add the fish, spoon the sauce over it, cover the casserole, and cook over medium-low heat for about 12 minutes, or until the fish is opaque and just flaking.

Transfer the fish strips to a dish with a spatula and turn the heat to high to reduce the sauce slightly. Stir in the parsley and pour the sauce over the fish. Serve immediately.

DESSERTS

POTATO DUMPLINGS WITH PRUNE AND NUT FILLING

KARTOPHELNYE VARENIKY

◆ ◆ ◆

Potatoes have a revered place in the East European kitchen, and are exploited fully. These dumplings are a specialty of the lower Ukraine and Moldova.

MAKES 32–36

- ◆ 1 3/4 lb floury potatoes, cooked, peeled, mashed and cooled
- ◆ 1 3/4–2 cups plain flour
- ◆ 1/3 cup shortening
- ◆ 1 egg yolk
- ◆ salt
- ◆ 1/4 tsp cinnamon
- ◆ 12 tbsp fresh breadcrumbs, toasted
- ◆ 1/2 cup sugar

For the filling

- ◆ 15 ready-to-eat prunes
- ◆ 1/2 tsp grated lemon rind
- ◆ 1 tbsp lemon juice
- ◆ 1/3 cup walnuts, finely chopped
- ◆ 1/4 cup sugar

Make the filling first. In a saucepan, just submerge the prunes in water. Bring to the boil, then lower the heat and simmer for 20 minutes. Cool the prunes in the liquid, then drain them, reserving 2 tbsp of the liquid. Stone and chop the prunes, place in a bowl, and mix together with the lemon rind and juice, walnuts, and sugar.

In a large bowl, beat the potatoes with 1 3/4 cups of the flour, the shortening, egg yolk, and salt to taste. Use your hands to work the mixture into a dough. Transfer to a floured surface and knead, adding a little more flour if necessary to get a smooth, glossy dough. Roll out until it is a large rectangle 1/3 in thick, then cut into squares of about 3 1/2 in.

Place a heaped teaspoon of the filling in the center of each square. Pull up the corners to enclose the filling, and form the dough around it to make a ball.

Bring a large saucepan of salted water to the boil, drop in the dumplings and poach for about 25 minutes, or until they are glossy and float to the surface.

Drain the dumplings thoroughly. Mix together the cinnamon, breadcrumbs and sugar, and roll the warm dumplings in the mixture. Serve immediately with soured cream.

Potato Dumplings with Prune and Nut Filling

ORANGES WITH SPICED RUM

APYELSINY V ROMYE Z PRYANOSTYAMI

◆ ◆ ◆

While vodka is the most common strong spirit of the people, *rhum* has always been used in cooking.

SERVES 6

◆ ¹/₂ cup sugar
◆ 2 tsp whole cloves
◆ 1¹/₂ cups water
◆ 2 tbsp dark rum
◆ 4–5 oranges, peeled, pith removed, and sliced

In a large saucepan, bring the sugar, cloves, and water to the boil. Continue to cook at medium-high heat until reduced by a quarter, and quite syrupy. Remove from the heat and stir in the rum. Leave to cool.

Place the sliced fruit in 6 individual glass bowls, and pour over the rum syrup. Chill for a couple of hours before serving.

SPICED HONEY CAKE

MEDIVNYK

◆ ◆ ◆

This delicious cake should be made at least 3 days ahead to let the flavors mature. It is a traditional part of Christmas festivities – celebrated with more ceremony in Catholic parts of the Ukraine and Belorussia than in Orthodox Russia, though honey cake is very popular there too.

SERVES 12

◆ 1 cup plus 1 tbsp dark honey
◆ 1 tsp cinnamon
◆ ¹/₂ tsp ground nutmeg
◆ ¹/₂ tsp ground cardamom
◆ 2 tsp baking soda
◆ ¹/₂ cup unsalted butter, softened
◆ 1 cup dark brown sugar
◆ 4 eggs at room temperature, separated
◆ ¹/₂ cup Greek- or Bulgarian-style yogurt
◆ ¹/₂ cup cottage cheese
◆ 1 tbsp freshly grated orange rind
◆ 2¹/₂ cups plain flour
◆ ¹/₂ tsp salt
◆ ¹/₃ cup plus 1 heaped tbsp raisins
◆ 6 oz ready-to-eat dates, stoned and finely chopped
◆ 1 cup walnuts, finely chopped

Place 1 cup honey, the cinnamon, nutmeg, and cardamom in a saucepan and bring to the boil over medium heat, stirring with a wooden spoon. Stir in the baking soda and remove from the heat. Cool.

In a large bowl, beat together the butter and brown sugar until the mixture is fluffy. Beat in the egg yolks, one at a time, then slowly stir in the cooled honey mixture. In another bowl, combine the yogurt, cottage cheese, and grated orange rind.

Sift the flour and salt into the honey-egg mixture, alternating with the yogurt mixture, stirring after each addition. Retain ¹/₂ cup of the flour, and toss it in a bowl with the raisins, dates and walnuts. Then stir this dry mixture into the batter.

Preheat the oven to 300°F. Beat the egg whites in a bowl until they hold stiff peaks. Whisk 2 tbsp egg white into the batter, then gently fold in the remainder.

Pour the batter into a well-buttered 10 in tube or *kugelhumf* pan, lined with buttered waxed paper. Bake the cake for 1¹/₂ hours, or until a cocktail stick comes out clean.

Cool the cake in the pan on a rack for 15 minutes, then invert onto the rack and remove the paper. Brush the cake with 1 tbsp honey, and allow to cool completely before storing in an airtight container for at least 2 days before serving.

CRIMEAN ALMOND SQUARES

SEVASTOPOLSKOYE PYECHENYE

◆ ◆ ◆

These biscuit-cakes became popular in the West following the siege of Sebastopol (1854–55), one of the most bloody episodes of the Crimean War.

MAKES 16 SQUARES

- ◆ *2 cups plain flour*
- ◆ *¹/₃ cup powdered sugar*
- ◆ *salt*
- ◆ *¹/₂ cup plus 2 tbsp unsalted butter*
- ◆ *1 large egg, beaten*

For the topping

- ◆ *6 egg whites*
- ◆ *1¹/₄ cups light brown sugar*
- ◆ *¹/₄ tsp ground cinnamon*
- ◆ *¹/₄ tsp finely grated lemon rind*
- ◆ *1³/₄ cups slivered almonds*

Sift the flour into a large bowl, and stir in the sugar and a pinch of salt. Cut in the butter, and work with your hands until the mixture has the consistency of fine breadcrumbs. Add the egg, and stir until the mixture forms into a dough. Roll the dough in a little flour, wrap in plastic wrap and chill for 1 hour.

Roll out the dough into a large square on floured waxed paper until it is as thin as possible. Trim the dough on the paper until it measures 12 x 12 in, then fit the paper and rolled dough into a 10 x 10 in baking pan. Push down the dough until you have a small rim (about ¹/₂ in). Prick the pastry all over with a fork, and chill for 1 hour.

Preheat the oven to 375°F. Bake the pastry blind for 15 minutes by lining it with greased aluminum foil and weighting it down with baking beans or rice. Remove the baking beans or rice and the foil, and bake for a further 5–8 minutes, or until the pastry is light gold. Leave to cool in the pan on a wire rack for 15 minutes, then lift out the pastry, remove from the lining paper, and place on a baking tray.

In a saucepan, combine the egg whites, sugar, cinnamon, lemon rind and almonds. Stir gently over high heat, without letting it boil, until the mixture is thickened and starts to become opaque. Pour the mixture into the pastry shell and bake for a further 25 minutes, or until the filling is set and browned. Serve warm or at room temperature, cut into squares.

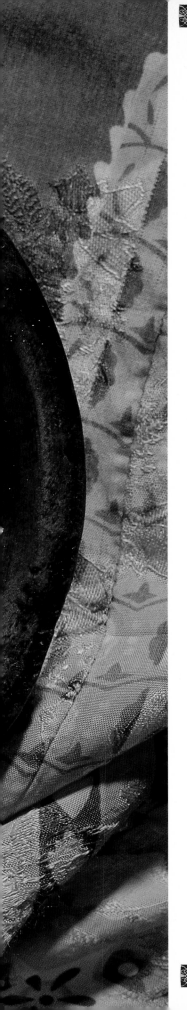

5

FROM SUNNY LANDS
BETWEEN THE SEAS
Georgia, Armenia,
and Azerbaijan

THE THREE TRANSCAUCASIAN REPUBLICS

HAVE SOME OF THE MOST VARIED SCENERY AND PEOPLES

OF THE OLD SOVIET NETWORK. TODAY, THEY ARE ALSO

EXPERIENCING SOME OF THE MOST VIOLENT UPHEAVALS, AS

DECADES OF REPRESSION GIVE WAY TO DIVERGING

POLITICAL ASPIRATIONS AND THE RE-EMERGENCE OF

LONG-HELD RIVALRIES BETWEEN ETHNIC AND

RELIGIOUS GROUPS.

The diversity of these regions has deep historical roots, since the lands have been successively fought over by Greeks, Romans, Persians, Byzantines, Arabs, Tartars, Turks and hundreds of smaller tribal groups, in turns rebuffed and assimilated by the native Caucasians (whose descendents are primarily Georgians) and Indo-Europeans (today mainly Armenians). This unsettled background is recognized by the contemporary existence of minority enclaves, the larger masquerading as "autonomous oblasts" – such as Nagorny-Karabakh in Azerbaijan, and South Ossetia on the borders of Georgia – and the smaller enduring less publicized, but often as abrasive, relations with their neighbors.

In the uncertain present, this cultural and religious *mélange* has proved a recipe for political and social disaster, but in happier times the fertile landbridge between the Black and Caspian Seas has guaranteed its varied inhabitants an example of the good life much

Armenian brandy is always checked carefully for color, bouquet, and taste.

A triumphant Azerbaijani fisherman holds aloft a sturgeon netted in the Caspian Sea.

envied by other Soviet states, who have to pay top prices for Caucasian produce exported to the markets of Moscow, St. Petersburg and other urban centers. In the Russian popular view, it is an exotic paradise full of sunshine, plenty, and the whiff of spice, whose citizens, even under the most oppressive regimes, have always engineered things their own way. Such is their confident spirit in these changing times that while Armenia and Azerbaijan have elected to stay within the new CIS, Georgia has decided to go her own way.

On the face of it, Georgia certainly has the most going for it of the three. It is the least culturally fractured – albeit riven, like the other two, by cataclysmic earthquakes. The rugged beauty of the Georgian countryside is complemented by the bounty of game – mountain goat, deer, boar, partridge, quail, and mountain turkey – while the streams meandering through mountain gorges and the limpid lakes shelter trout, carp, barbel, and the secretive *kramuli*, found only there. Wild and cultivated fruit grows in profusion; vegetables could be champion entries in any fair in the West, yet lose nothing of their succulence and flavor with their size. The fame of Georgian wine has assured that it is one product associated with the region in the international subconscious.

Georgians tend to be proud, clever, and high-spirited; they love feasting and merrymaking, but do not suffer fools gladly. Traditional houses are bright in pastel shades; this – together with the frequency of classical columns – gives them a character strangely reminiscent of ancient Cretan reconstructions, except for the wooden galleries running around the upper stories. In summer, there are vine-shaded corners with tables permanently erected for impromptu visits from family and friends – always an occasion for eating and drinking.

Armenia is achingly beautiful, too, if perhaps more austerely so; only 1 percent of its land is lower than 3,300 ft above sea level. Disasters, natural and man-made, have stalked its history, so its people have had to be survivors. Their business acumen has stood them in good stead in their diaspora throughout Europe and America – a flight prompted by pogroms in their ancestral homelands, which stretch across the Turkish border, and by closure of their schools, newspapers, and churches by the Soviet authorities. Famed as farmers, stonemasons and horsebreeders at home, they have won a reputation as antique dealers, jewelers, haberdashers, and restaurateurs abroad.

Both Armenia and Georgia have their own national Orthodox churches with similarly ornate, if distinct, liturgies, though there are also a large number of Armenian Catholics, who follow the Orthodox rite but swear allegiance to the Pope.

There are many overt similarities between the cuisines of Georgia and Armenia, which also echo the cooking styles of Turkey, the Balkans, and the Middle East. The delight in the combination of colorful vegetables and peppers, most notably in Armenian *ghivetch*; in vegetables and vine leaves stuffed with combinations of meat and/or rice; in the dominance of lamb – and of grilled meats in general; in the popularity of nuts and dried fruits, and of eggplant "caviar" and pulses (*lobio/loubia*) stewed in herby tomato sauces; in the use of yogurt in sweet and spicy dishes. Often made from the fermented milk of the water buffalo, yogurt is known as *matsoni* in Georgia and *matsun* in Armenia.

But there are subtle, and more apparent, differences within these general tastes. While Georgian pilafs are usually made with rice, those of Armenia as often contain cracked wheat (*bulgur*). Both nationalities love walnuts – but for the Georgians they are a passion. Armenians might well replace them in a recipe with pinenuts. The flat cracker bread, known as *lavash* in Armenia, adds an "i" in Georgia (*lavashi*) as well as yeast to become a puffy bread in the Lebanese and Syrian tradition. The Georgian taste for wild foods is satisfied by nettles and sarsaparilla in soups and wild purslane (*donduri*) in salads; the sour-sweet tang of tarragon can often be detected in their favorite dishes. Armenians look to pumpkin, pomegranate, and sesame seeds to provide a special fillip to food, while the slightly acrid bite of coriander (cilantro) supplants that of tarragon. And while the Georgians toast their happiness in wine and champagne, the Armenians raise their brandy glasses.

The republic of Azerbaijan is an impressionistic mixture of traditions, and one that has seen little of non-Russian tourism. Though ethnically and linguistically Turkish, its style of life is a reflection of that in Central Asia on the other side of the Caspian Sea. Its food, on the other hand, borrows liberally from both the Georgian and Central Asian traditions. *Pilaf* and lamb kebab (*shashlyk*) recall the former, while yogurt soups and dumplings have an Uzbek flavor. And, as in Uzbekistan, social life in Muslim Azerbaijan revolves largely around the teahouse, or *chaikhana*.

General view of the 16th to 18th century temples and fortress at Annanuri in rural Georgia.

ONION, SPLIT PEA, AND LEMON SOUP
SUP IZ LUKA, GOROKHA I LIMONA

◆ ◆ ◆

Barley and lentils are two Armenian favorites paired in this earthy soup. Served with warm cornbread, it would make a filling supper or lunch.

SERVES 6

- *1 cup water*
- *$^1/_3$ cup plus 1 tbsp pearl barley*
- *1 tbsp tomato paste*
- *$6^1/_4$ cups beef stock*
- *$^3/_4$ cup brown split peas, rinsed and picked over*
- *5 onions, sliced very thinly*
- *1 tsp dried anise seeds*
- *juice of 1 large lemon*
- *large pinch of sweet paprika*
- *pinch of cayenne pepper*
- *salt and freshly ground black pepper*
- *12 paper-thin lemon slices*

Bring the water to the boil in a large enamelled or stainless steel saucepan. Stir in the barley, cover, and simmer over low heat for about 20–25 minutes, until the barley is just tender and the water has been absorbed. Stir in the tomato paste, beef stock, split peas, onions, and anise. Bring to the boil, cover, and simmer over low heat for 1 hour, or until the lentils are soft.

Stir in the lemon juice, paprika, cayenne pepper, and salt and pepper to taste, and simmer uncovered for a further 20 minutes. Pour the soup into heated bowls, and garnish each with two very thin slices of lemon.

SPICED PUMPKIN SOUP

TYKVENNY SUP Z PRYANOSTYAMI

◆ ◆ ◆

Pumpkins grow in profusion throughout the southern states of the former Soviet Union. They are a cheap source of vitamins, and are served baked, stewed, stuffed, in pastries, and in soups like this Armenian specialty. Nothing is wasted – even the seeds are roasted and treated as snack food or a condiment to sprinkle over dishes. The yogurt in this soup would be *matsun*, made from water-buffalo milk.

SERVES 8

- ◆ 3 tbsp pumpkin seeds
- ◆ 3 tbsp vegetable oil
- ◆ $^1/_3$ cup currants
- ◆ $^1/_2$ lb leeks, trimmed, halved, and thinly sliced
- ◆ 2 medium carrots, peeled and finely chopped

- ◆ $1^1/_2$ lb fresh pumpkin, peeled, seeded, fiber removed, and cubed
- ◆ $4^1/_3$ cups chicken stock
- ◆ $1^3/_4$ cups milk
- ◆ $^1/_4$ tsp allspice
- ◆ $^2/_3$ cup yogurt

Preheat the oven to 400°F. Place the pumpkin seeds on a baking tray and toast in the oven for 5–6 minutes, or until they are golden. Set aside.

Heat the oil in a saucepan, and stir the currants over medium heat until they are puffed and glossy. Transfer with a slotted spoon to a plate and set aside. Stir the leeks and carrots into the pan and cook over low heat for 10 minutes, then add the pumpkin cubes and stir-fry for another 10 minutes until the leeks are lightly colored. Add $1^3/_4$ cups chicken stock. Cover and cook the vegetables for 20 minutes, or until the pumpkin is softened.

In a blender or food processor, purée the vegetable mixture in batches until smooth. Return the purée to the saucepan and stir in the remaining stock, the milk, and the allspice. Cook over medium heat, covered, for 15 minutes, stirring occasionally. Stir in the currants just before serving.

Serve the soup in individual bowls. Top each serving with a swirl of yogurt, and sprinkle with some toasted pumpkin seeds.

SOUR CHICKEN SOUP

CHIKHIRTMA

◆ ◆ ◆

A traditional Georgian soup, this has echoes of Syria, Israel, and the Indian subcontinent in it. If a thicker, more stew-like result is wanted, the chicken can be shredded into the broth, but this version is more like that commonly encountered in Tbilisi *kafes* and *restorans*.

SERVES 8

- ◆ *4 lb chicken, gutted and cleaned*
- ◆ *1 whole onion, unpeeled*
- ◆ *1 celery stick*
- ◆ *3–4 saffron threads*
- ◆ *5 black peppercorns, crushed*
- ◆ *pinch of cayenne pepper*
- ◆ *3 eggs*
- ◆ *2 egg yolks*
- ◆ *2 tbsp unsalted butter*
- ◆ *2 onions, finely chopped*
- ◆ *1 tbsp flour*
- ◆ *$1/_2$ cup fresh lemon juice*
- ◆ *2 tbsp finely chopped fresh coriander (cilantro)*
- ◆ *2 tbsp finely chopped fresh parsley*
- ◆ *1 tbsp finely chopped fresh mint*
- ◆ *salt and freshly ground black pepper*

Place the chicken, whole onion, and celery stick in a heavy saucepan. Add cold water to cover well, and bring to the boil over high heat. Add the saffron, peppercorns and cayenne pepper to taste, then cover and lower the heat to minimum. Simmer gently for $1^1/_2$ hours, or until the bird is tender but not falling to pieces. During cooking, skim the scum from the top of the stock occasionally.

Transfer the chicken to a dish to drain. Add the juices to the stock. Reserve the bird for another use, serving it with Spiced Walnut Sauce or using it in Russian Chicken and Potato Salad.

Remove the peppercorns and any bits from the stock with a small sieve, but keep it simmering. In a large bowl, lightly beat together the eggs and egg yolks. Melt the butter in a frying pan over medium heat. Sauté the onions until they are softened and just colored, about 6–8 minutes. Add the flour and stir for 3 minutes. Add $1^1/_4$ cups stock to the frying pan and stir until it begins to thicken. Take off the heat, and allow to rest for 2 minutes, then pour the thickened mixture slowly into the eggs, beating all the time. In turn, pour the egg and stock mixture and the lemon juice into the rest of the stock, beating gently over low heat so that it does not curdle. Stir in the chopped herbs, season the soup to taste, and serve immediately.

SATSIVI SAUCE

◆ ◆ ◆

This is the best-known classic sauce of the Georgian repertoire, although it is probably more familiar in its Turkish incarnation, Circassian Sauce. As in Turkey, it is usually paired with poached chicken, but the addition of breadcrumbs and heavier spicing in the Turkish version results in a less vibrant sauce than the recipe below.

MAKES ABOUT $2^1/_2$ CUPS

- ◆ *$1^1/_2$ cups shelled walnuts*
- ◆ *4 cloves garlic, crushed and chopped*
- ◆ *$1^1/_2$ cups chicken stock*
- ◆ *2 tbsp chicken fat or clarified butter*
- ◆ *2 medium onions, finely chopped*
- ◆ *1 bay leaf*
- ◆ *$1/_2$ tsp coriander seeds*
- ◆ *$1/_4$ tsp cinnamon*
- ◆ *$1/_4$ tsp turmeric*
- ◆ *large pinch of ground cloves*
- ◆ *large pinch of cayenne pepper*
- ◆ *2 tbsp red wine vinegar*
- ◆ *salt and freshly ground black pepper*
- ◆ *2 tsp finely chopped tarragon*
- ◆ *2 tsp finely chopped flat-leaved parsley*

In a food processor fitted with a metal blade, process the nuts and garlic until they are as smooth as possible (or grind by hand using a mortar and pestle). Add 1 tsp chicken stock, if needed.

In a heavy enamelled or stainless steel saucepan, melt the chicken fat or clarified butter. Cook the onions over low heat until softened but not colored, about 5 minutes. Stir in the walnut-garlic mixture, the bay leaf, and the chicken stock. Bring to the boil, then lower the heat and simmer for 15 minutes, until reduced and thickened. Stir in the spices, vinegar, seasoning to taste, and 1 tsp each of the herbs, reserving the rest. Transfer to a bowl to cool, then chill for 2 hours. Serve with the remaining herbs scattered over the top.

BAKU TOMATO PRESERVE

KONSERVIROVANNYE TOMATY PO-BAKINSKY

◆ ◆ ◆

This highly flavored chutney is a good accompaniment to the fish and lamb dishes common to the Azerbaijani and Georgian regions.

MAKES ABOUT 2 ½ CUPS

- ◆ *1 red sweet pepper, cored, seeded, and finely chopped*
- ◆ *1 yellow sweet pepper, cored, seeded, and finely chopped*
- ◆ *2 thin green hot chillies, seeded, trimmed, and finely chopped*
- ◆ *2 beefsteak tomatoes, skinned, cored, seeded, and chopped*
- ◆ *1 onion, chopped*
- ◆ *1 tsp sugar*
- ◆ *salt*
- ◆ *1 tbsp red wine vinegar*

Combine all the ingredients in a glass or pottery bowl and mix well. Cover with plastic wrap and leave to marinate for 3–24 hours.

GEORGIAN POMEGRANATE CHUTNEY

GRUZINSKAYA GRANATOVAYA PODLIVKA

◆ ◆ ◆

This pomegranate chutney is delicious with fish and with grilled lamb.

MAKES ABOUT 1 CUP

- ◆ *seeds from 2 medium pomegranates*
- ◆ *1 orange, peeled, pith removed, and cut into pieces*
- ◆ *2 tsp fresh lime or lemon juice*
- ◆ *2 scallions, trimmed and finely chopped*
- ◆ *¼ tsp mixed cayenne pepper and sweet paprika*
- ◆ *2 tsp finely chopped fresh hot chilli*
- ◆ *1 tbsp finely chopped fresh coriander (cilantro)*

Combine all the ingredients in a glass or pottery bowl, and stir to mix thoroughly. Cover and chill for 3–12 hours.

GEORGIAN CHEESE-FILLED BREADS
KHACHAPURI

◆ ◆ ◆

This delicious bread is made in a variety of ways in its home territory. Round, filled loaves are probably the most common presentation, while some other versions have layered pastry. These open-faced 'buns' are easily frozen if they are not all needed at once. In Georgia the cheese used would be *suluguni*, a cheese rather like Turkish *halloumi*.

MAKES ABOUT 16–18

- ◆ *$^1/_4$ cup plus 1 tbsp unsalted butter, softened*
- ◆ *1 cup lukewarm water*
- ◆ *$2^1/_2$ tsp (1 x $^1/_4$ oz packet) active dry yeast*
- ◆ *2 tsp sugar*
- ◆ *$2^1/_2$ cups plain flour*
- ◆ *1 tsp salt*
- ◆ *1 lb* halloumi *cheese, grated*
- ◆ *2 eggs*
- ◆ *2 tbsp finely chopped oregano, marjoram, or tarragon*

In a small saucepan, heat 3 tbsp butter over a low heat until only just melted. Allow to cool.

Place the water in a small bowl and sprinkle the yeast and sugar into it. Leave for 15 minutes in a warm place, or until foamy. In a large bowl, mix together 2 cups flour and the salt. Make a well in the center, and pour in the yeast and the melted butter; stir with a fork until you have a pliable dough.

Transfer the dough to a floured surface and knead with your hands for 5 minutes, adding the remaining flour as you work the dough. When the dough is no longer sticky but smooth and still soft, transfer it to a well-buttered bowl and turn it to coat with the butter. Leave it to rise in a warm place, covered with plastic wrap, for about 1 hour, or until doubled in size.

In another bowl, stir together the grated cheese, 1 egg, and the remaining softened butter. Work the mixture well with your hands and set aside.

Knock back the dough, halve it, and roll one half into a 16 x 8 in rectangle. Divide the rectangle into squares. Use half the cheese mixture to make mounds in the center of the squares and fold the sides up around and slightly over the mixture, pulling out the corners slightly. Repeat with remaining dough and cheese mixture.

Preheat the oven to 375°F. Make an egg wash by mixing the remaining egg with a little water in a small bowl. Arrange the filled bread cases on two baking trays and brush with the egg wash. Allow them to rest for 15 minutes in a warm place, then bake in the oven for 20–25 minutes, or until they are golden and the cheese is toasted. Transfer to a rack, sprinkle with the fresh herbs, and leave to cool for 15 minutes before serving warm. (The *khachapuri* may be frozen and reheated at the same temperature for 25 minutes from frozen.)

KARABAKH-STYLE SALAD

SALAT PO-KARABAKHSKY

◆ ◆ ◆

This light mixed salad is characteristic of the eastern reaches of the Caucasian Republic which borders on the Caspian Sea. The Armenian version is almost the same, but substitutes 2 tomatoes for the radishes.

SERVES 4

- 1 bunch of radishes, trimmed and thinly sliced
- 1 small cucumber, peeled, seeded, and thinly sliced
- 3 scallions, trimmed and chopped
- 2 tsp finely chopped fresh mint
- 3 tbsp fresh lemon juice
- 3 tbsp olive oil
- $^1/_4$ lb fresh ewe's or feta cheese, cubed
- salt and freshly ground black pepper

Combine the radishes, cucumber, scallions, and fresh mint in an attractive bowl. Whisk the lemon juice and oil together and season to taste. Pour over the salad and toss gently. Scatter the cubes of cheese around the edges of the bowl and serve immediately.

Stuffed Vine Leaves

STUFFED VINE LEAVES

YARPAKH DOLMASY

◆ ◆ ◆

Both Armenians and Georgians love stuffed vine leaves – with or without meat. The Armenians are more likely to use *bulgur* rather than rice.

MAKES ABOUT 30

- ◆ ¹/₂ cup coarse bulgur (cracked wheat)
- ◆ 1³/₄ cup hot water
- ◆ 2 packets vine leaves in brine (about 30 leaves)
- ◆ ¹/₄ cup olive oil
- ◆ scant ¹/₂ cup pine nuts
- ◆ 2 small onions, finely chopped
- ◆ ¹/₂ lb lean ground lamb
- ◆ ¹/₃ cup currants
- ◆ 6-7 ready-to-eat dried apricots, finely chopped
- ◆ 2 tbsp chopped fresh dill
- ◆ 2 tbsp chopped fresh mint
- ◆ salt and freshly ground black pepper
- ◆ 1 cup chicken stock
- ◆ 2–3 lemons, quartered
- ◆ 2¹/₂ cups Greek- or Bulgarian-style yogurt
- ◆ ground cinnamon

Place the bulgur in a large bowl and add the hot water. Leave to soak for 30 minutes.

Meanwhile place the vine leaves in another large bowl, cover them with cold water, and leave them to soak for 20 minutes, or until they will pull apart easily. Drain, pour fresh water into the bowl, and drain again thoroughly. Spread the vine leaves out and pat them dry with paper towels. Drain the bulgur in a fine sieve or through cheesecloth.

Heat the oil in a heavy frying pan over moderate heat. Add the pine nuts and toast, stirring, until golden. Transfer with a slotted spoon to a plate and set aside. Add the onions to the oil and sauté gently until they are soft and just coloring, about 8 minutes. Add the lamb and sauté, stirring, until browned. Add the currants, apricots, herbs, seasoning to taste, pine nuts, bulgur, and lemon juice; heat until warmed through.

Take a vine leaf and place it stem-side facing you on a flat surface. Spoon a scant tablespoon of stuffing in the center of the leaf. Trim off the stem, tuck the sides over the filling, and roll away from you to form a tight, neat roll. Repeat with the remaining stuffing and leaves. Arrange the stuffed rolls, seam-side down, in a flameproof casserole large enough to take them in one tight layer. Add the stock and enough hot water to come halfway up the sides of the rolls. Place the casserole over high heat and bring to the boil. Cover, and simmer over minimum heat for about 40 minutes.

Remove from the heat, uncover, and let the rolls cool to room temperature, then chill if desired. (The rolls will keep in the refrigerator, well-covered with plastic wrap, for 3 days).

Serve the rolls garnished with lemon quarters, and with a bowl of thick yogurt sprinkled with cinnamon.

SPINACH AND WALNUT PURÉE

PKHALA

◆ ◆ ◆

This spiced spinach dish is a common offering at Georgian *zakuska* tables. Armenians substitute lemon juice and toasted pine nuts for the vinegar and walnuts. It is scooped up in flat, flaky *lavashi* (or Armenian *lavash*) bread, with yogurt accompanying it if desired.

SERVES 4–6

- ◆ 3 lb spinach leaves, washed and coarse stems removed
- ◆ 1 small onion, chopped
- ◆ 1 tbsp olive oil
- ◆ 3 cloves garlic, crushed
- ◆ 5 threads saffron
- ◆ 1 tbsp hot water
- ◆ handful fresh coriander, (cilantro) coarse stems removed
- ◆ handful fresh flat-leaved parsley, coarse stems removed
- ◆ 2 tbsp red wine vinegar or lemon juice
- ◆ ³/₄ cup shelled walnuts or toasted pine nuts
- ◆ salt and freshly ground black pepper
- ◆ ²/₃ cup chicken stock
- ◆ extra chopped walnuts or toasted whole pine nuts

Place the spinach in a large saucepan and cook in the moisture clinging to its leaves, stirring occasionally, until it is wilted – about 8 minutes. Squeeze the spinach to remove as much water as possible, and allow to drain further.

In a frying pan, sauté the onion in the olive oil until it is soft. Stir in the garlic, and cook over medium heat for 2–3 more minutes, but do not let the garlic brown. Meanwhile, soak the saffron threads in the hot water.

Squeeze the spinach again to remove excess water, and chop it coarsely. In a blender or processor, combine the spinach, the contents of the frying pan, and the fresh coriander and parsley. Process until smooth. Transfer to a bowl, together with the saffron and its liquid, and the vinegar or lemon juice.

Using the grinder attachment of the blender or the cleaned bowl of the food processor, process the walnuts or pine nuts until finely chopped but not mashed. Stir into the spinach mixture with seasoning and as much of the chicken stock as is needed to make a stiffish purée. Spoon the purée into a serving dish, smooth the top with the prongs of a fork, and leave to stand, covered with plastic wrap, for at least 3 hours for the flavors to combine. Scatter over a handful of chopped walnuts or toasted pine nuts just before serving.

EGGPLANT CAVIAR

BAKLAZHANNYA IKRA

◆ ◆ ◆

The smoky flavor of this Georgian "caviar" has become familiar to Westerners through Lebanese and Turkish restaurants, which also serve versions of this classic dip. An Armenian version, known as *babaghanouj*, adds green pepper and pomegranate seeds, shown as options below.

SERVES 6

- ◆ *2 lb eggplant, trimmed and halved lengthways*
- ◆ *salt and freshly ground black pepper*
- ◆ *4 tbsp olive oil*
- ◆ *5 scallions, trimmed and finely chopped*
- ◆ *1 green sweet pepper, cored, seeded, and chopped (optional)*
- ◆ *2 cloves garlic, crushed and finely chopped*
- ◆ *2 ripe tomatoes, skinned, seeded, and chopped*
- ◆ *pinch of cayenne pepper*
- ◆ *1 tbsp fresh lemon juice*
- ◆ *3 tbsp finely chopped fresh coriander (cilantro) or parsley*
- ◆ *seeds from 1 pomegranate (optional)*

Slash the eggplant on the sides, and sprinkle with salt all over. Place in a colander and let them drain for 30 minutes. Rinse the eggplant, and pat them dry with absorbent paper towels.

Preheat the oven to 375°F. Place the eggplant on a baking tray, cut side down, and brush all over with oil. Bake in the oven for 40 minutes, until very tender. Remove from the oven to cool.

Meanwhile, place 2 tbsp olive oil in a frying pan. Add the scallions, and the green pepper if used, and stir for 5 minutes until soft. Add the garlic and cook for another minute.

When the eggplant is cool, scrape out the flesh and chop it finely. Add the rest of the oil to the pan and stir in the chopped eggplant, together with the tomatoes, cayenne pepper, and seasoning to taste. Turn the heat to high and bring the mixture to boiling point, mashing and stirring it at the same time. Cover, lower the heat and simmer, stirring occasionally, for about 30 minutes, or until the mixture has thickened and most of the moisture has evaporated. Stir in the lemon juice and coriander (substitute parsley and add the pomegranate seeds if making *babaghanouj*), adjust the seasoning, and transfer the mixture to a bowl to cool. Leave to stand for at least 3 hours; serve at room temperature. (The caviar may be kept, chilled, for up to 3 days.)

TRANSCAUCASIAN CABBAGE AND MINT SALAD

TRANSCARKAZSKY SALAT IZ KAPUSTY Z MYATOY

◆ ◆ ◆

Cabbage is a staple of the former Soviet Union, but in the south the spicing is notably different, and sour cream gives way to yogurt, when used. This is a cool, refreshing "coleslaw" served as a *zakuska* or to accompany a picnic or outdoor meal.

SERVES 6–8

- ◆ *1¹⁄₂ tbsp lemon juice*
- ◆ *2 tbsp white wine vinegar*
- ◆ *1¹⁄₂ tbsp sunflower or olive oil*
- ◆ *¹⁄₂ tsp sugar*
- ◆ *freshly ground black pepper*
- ◆ *1 large red onion*
- ◆ *2¹⁄₂ lb white Dutch cabbage, outer leaves removed, cored, quartered, and finely shredded*
- ◆ *6 tbsp finely shredded fresh mint leaves*

Beat together the lemon juice and vinegar in a large bowl. Whisk in the oil, sugar, and a generous dash of pepper. Halve and finely slice all but one-quarter of the red onion. Stir the onion slices into the dressing, and wrap the remaining section in aluminum foil. Then gently toss the shredded cabbage and mint leaves in the dressing. Combine thoroughly, and chill for at least 3 hours.

Just before serving, slice the reserved onion and sprinkle over the salad.

VEGETABLES

ARMENIAN VEGETABLE STEW

GHIVETCH

◆ ◆ ◆

There are no hard and fast rules to making this very Armenian specialty. It can contain meat to make it more substantial – tender pieces of lamb sautéed before adding the vegetables – while the latter are an amalgam of whatever is in the refrigerator, for example, substitute turnip for carrots, cabbage for celery.

SERVES 4–6

- ◆ ¹/₃ cup plus 1 tbsp olive oil
- ◆ 4 cloves garlic, crushed
- ◆ 1 cup beef stock or consommé
- ◆ 1 bay leaf
- ◆ ¹/₂ tsp dried tarragon
- ◆ ¹/₂ tsp dried oregano
- ◆ salt and freshly ground black pepper
- ◆ 2 medium carrots, halved and thinly sliced
- ◆ ¹/₄ lb fresh stringless green beans, cut into ¹/₂ in lengths
- ◆ 2 small potatoes, peeled and diced
- ◆ 2 celery sticks, halved lengthways and thinly sliced
- ◆ 1 zucchini, thinly sliced into rounds
- ◆ 1 small eggplant, halved and thinly sliced
- ◆ 1 small red onion, thinly sliced
- ◆ 1 small cauliflower, broken into florets
- ◆ ¹/₂ red sweet pepper, cored, seeded, and cut into strips
- ◆ ¹/₂ green sweet pepper, cored, seeded, and cut into strips
- ◆ ³/₄ cup shelled fresh peas

Preheat the oven to 350°F. Place the oil in a large enamelled or stainless steel casserole and warm it over medium heat. Add the garlic and stir to flavor the oil, about 2 minutes. Pour in the beef stock or consommé and add the bay leaf, herbs, and seasoning to taste. Bring to the boil.

Add the vegetables, little by little, stirring to combine as you add them. Cover the casserole with a lid or foil, and transfer to the oven. Bake for about 1 hour or until the vegetables are all tender, stirring occasionally. Serve as a vegetarian main course or as a side dish.

F I S H

SEVAN LAKE TROUT YEREVAN-STYLE
SEVANSKAYA FOREL PO-YEREVANSKY

◆ ◆ ◆

**Said to be the most delicious in Armenia, Sevan Lake
trout can sometimes be found in the market at Yerevan,
46 miles to the southwest of the lake. The capital's market is
richer in vegetables and herbs than is the norm. This recipe
combines the flavors of that region, though
we cannot duplicate the unique lake fish.**

SERVES 4

- *³/₄ lb brown or rainbow trout, cleaned and gutted*
- *salt and freshly ground black pepper*
- *¹/₄ cup unsalted butter*
- *8 oz bottled artichoke hearts in oil*
- *¹/₂ cup plain flour*
- *²/₃ cup fresh lemon juice*
- *1 cup water*

- *¹/₃ cup plus 1 tbsp vegetable oil*
- *1¹/₂ tbsp dry white wine*
- *3 tbsp drained capers*
- *3 tbsp finely chopped fresh flat-leaved parsley*
- *pinch of sweet paprika*
- *small pinch of cayenne pepper*

Rinse the trout and pat it dry with paper towels. Season to taste and set aside.

In a heavy saucepan over low heat, gently melt the butter until the solids have sunk to the bottom of the pan. Slowly pour off the clarified butter on the top and set aside. Discard the white residue and wash the pan.

Pour the oil from the bottled artichokes into the saucepan. Add 1 tsp flour and heat over a medium flame, stirring. Slowly add half the lemon juice and the water, and bring the liquid to the boil, whisking. Lower the heat to simmer, stir in the artichoke hearts and cook, uncovered, for about 10 minutes, or until the sauce is reduced and thickened. Set aside.

Preheat the oven to 375°F. Dredge the trout in flour and shake off the excess. Heat half the oil in a frying pan, and brown two of the trout on one side only. Remove to a roasting pan lined with oiled foil, add the rest of the oil to the frying pan and brown the two remaining trout on one side. Transfer to the roasting pan. Bake the trout for 10 minutes, or until the flesh is opaque and just beginning to flake. Carefully fillet the trout, arrange on four warmed serving plates, and sprinkle the fillets with the wine.

Stir the remaining lemon juice, the clarified butter and the capers into the sauce, and heat through. Spoon the mixture over the fillets, and sprinkle with the chopped parsley and the spices. Serve immediately.

ARMENIAN-STYLE CHICKEN AND CHICKPEA STEW

TYSHYONY TSYPLYONOK Z GRUSHAMI PO-ARMYANSKY

◆ ◆ ◆

The Armenians have a spicy condiment sold as Aintab Red Pepper here in the West. Since it is difficult to find, two thin medium-hot red peppers have been substituted here.

SERVES 6

- 4 threads saffron
- scant ¹/₂ cup hot water
- 10 cloves garlic, crushed
- 2 fresh thin medium-hot red peppers, seeded and chopped
- 4 tbsp vegetable or sunflower oil
- 3 lb chicken breasts and thighs, washed and dried
- salt and freshly ground black pepper
- 2 tbsp ground coriander
- 1 tsp dried oregano
- 2 x 14 oz cans plum tomatoes, drained
- 1³/₄ cup plus 2 tbsp water
- 1¹/₄ lb can chickpeas, drained
- 2 tbsp lemon juice

Soak the saffron in hot water for 10 minutes. Place the saffron and liquid, garlic and peppers in a blender or food processor. Process until finely chopped and set aside.

Heat the oil in a casserole over medium-hot heat. Season the chicken to taste, and sauté in batches until lightly browned. Remove to a plate and keep warm.

Reduce the heat and add the crushed garlic. Stir with a wooden spoon for 2 minutes, then add the ground coriander and oregano. Stir for a further 2 minutes, then add the tomatoes. Break them up with the spoon while cooking for 3 minutes, then add the water. Add the chicken pieces and spoon the sauce over them. Bring to the boil, cover, and simmer over low heat for 20 minutes.

Add the chickpeas and continue to cook, covered, for a further 15 minutes. Remove the lid, stir in the lemon juice, and increase the heat. Boil for 5 minutes to reduce the sauce. Serve immediately.

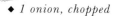

GEORGIAN LAMB CUBES ON SKEWERS

SHASHLYK

◆ ◆ ◆

Shashlyk is the Georgian name for what is more commonly known here by its Turkish title, *shish kebab*. Unlike the Muslims, however, the Orthodox Georgians marinate their lamb in their dry Telliani wine.

SERVES 6

- ◆ *1 onion, chopped*
- ◆ *¼ cup mixed olive oil and vegetable oil*
- ◆ *1 bay leaf*
- ◆ *1 clove garlic, crushed*
- ◆ *2 tbsp finely chopped flat-leaved parsley*
- ◆ *1 tsp dried oregano*
- ◆ *¼ tsp freshly ground black pepper*
- ◆ *large pinch cayenne pepper*
- ◆ *1 cup dry red wine*
- ◆ *2 lb lean boneless leg of lamb steak, cubed*
- ◆ *30 small white onions, peeled*
- ◆ *2 small red sweet peppers, cored, seeded, and cut into square pieces*

Place the onion, oils, bay leaf, garlic, parsley, oregano, pepper, and cayenne pepper in a thick plastic bag. Pour in

PHEASANT GEORGIAN-STYLE

PHAZAN PO-GRUZINSKY

◆ ◆ ◆

This dish is a relative of Walnut Chicken but has its own special accents. Made in its home region it would use sweet golden Gurdzhanni wine, but Madeira or *oloroso* sherry are acceptable substitutes.

SERVES 4

- ◆ $^3/_4$ cup boiling water
- ◆ 1 heaped tsp Turkish or other green tea leaves
- ◆ $1^1/_2$ lb green grapes, stems removed
- ◆ $2^1/_2$–3 lb pheasant, cleaned and trussed
- ◆ juice of 3 oranges
- ◆ 1 tsp grated orange rind
- ◆ $^1/_2$ cup walnuts, chopped
- ◆ 1 cup Madeira
- ◆ salt and freshly ground black pepper
- ◆ 3 tbsp butter
- ◆ $^1/_2$ cup game consommé
- ◆ quince jelly (optional)

Pour the boiling water over the tea and allow it to steep for 10 minutes, then strain. Set aside the liquid tea and discard the leaves.

In a large bowl, mash the grapes with a potato masher or pestle. Continue until they are a pulpy mass and there is plenty of juice. Strain the mixture, discard the pulp, and set aside the juice.

Place the pheasant in a Dutch oven or roasting pan with the orange rind and walnuts. Mix together the tea, grape juice, orange juice and Madeira, and pour over the pheasant. Season to taste, and dot the bird with butter. Cover with a lid or foil, and bring the braising liquid to the boil on top of the hob. Reduce the heat and simmer for 45–50 minutes.

Preheat the oven to 425°F. Lift out the pheasant and place it on a dish to drain. Strain the cooking liquid into a saucepan and discard the solids. Place the saucepan over medium-high heat and reduce until it is thick and syrupy, about 8 minutes. Carve the bird into serving pieces, and return to the roasting pan. Cook uncovered for 20 minutes, or until it has browned lightly.

Transfer the pheasant to a serving dish. Pour the reduced stock over the pieces and serve immediately. Serve accompanied by a bowl of quince jelly, if available.

the wine. Hold tightly shut and shake vigorously to combine. Add the cubed lamb, tie the bag closed, and place it in a bowl large enough to contain it comfortably. Leave for 24–36 hours in the refrigerator to mature.

Drain the lamb well, but reserve the marinade. Thread the pieces onto 6 long skewers, alternating with the onions and red pepper.

Prepare the coals of a barbecue or preheat a grill. When ready, lay the skewers about 5 in from the heat. Cook, turning once or twice and basting frequently, for about 10 minutes, or until the lamb is still pink inside but well browned. Serve with rice and Baku Tomato Preserve .

GEORGIAN MEAT AND TOMATO STEW
CHAKHOBILI

◆ ◆ ◆

**This traditional dish is made as frequently with chicken
as it is with lamb. In the old manner, it is cooked in a large
iron pot over hot coals, but this version has been adapted
to suit the modern stove.**

SERVES 6

- ◆ *1 tbsp vegetable or olive oil*
- ◆ *2 lb lamb steaks, trimmed of fat and cubed*
- ◆ *2 onions, chopped*
- ◆ *1½ lb whole Roma or plum tomatoes, skinned, seeded, and roughly chopped*
- ◆ *3 large potatoes, peeled and roughly cubed*
- ◆ *salt and freshly ground black pepper*
- ◆ *handful fresh coriander (cilantro), chopped*
- ◆ *handful fresh flat-leaved parsley, chopped*
- ◆ *5 fresh basil leaves, chopped*
- ◆ *8 cloves garlic, crushed*

Heat the oil in a large enamelled or stainless steel casserole until very hot, but not smoking. Tilt to cover the bottom with the oil. Add the lamb pieces and brown, stirring with a wooden spoon, for 10 minutes. When the meat is colored, add the onions and continue to stir until they are soft. Add the tomatoes and use the spoon to crush them. Stir in the potatoes and seasoning to taste. Cover and simmer over low heat for about 45 minutes, or until the meat and potatoes are tender and the tomatoes have become a mushy sauce. Uncover and turn up the heat. Stir in the herbs and garlic and continue to stir as the sauce bubbles for 10 minutes. Take off the heat, cover, and leave to stand for 5–8 minutes before serving.

LOSH KIBBEH KEBABS

LOSH KIBBEHSKIYE KEBABY

◆ ◆ ◆

**The Azerbaijani version of this dish dispenses
with the *bulgur* and increases the ground meat, but the
spices and herbs are much the same. The Armenian
version is given here as the *bulgur* gives the dish a more
interesting texture.**

SERVES 4

- ◆ ½ *cup fine bulgur*
- ◆ *2 tbsp tomato paste*
- ◆ *1 lb lean minced lamb*
- ◆ *3 tbsp chopped onion*
- ◆ *3 tbsp chopped fresh flat-
  leaved parsley*
- ◆ ½ *tsp allspice*
- ◆ ¼ *tsp cayenne pepper*

- ◆ *salt and freshly ground
  black pepper*
- ◆ ½ *tsp grated lemon rind*
- ◆ *vegetable oil*
- ◆ *1 small red sweet pepper,
  cored, seeded, and sliced
  into rounds*

Place the *bulgur* in a bowl, add water to cover generously and leave to soak for 10–15 minutes, or until the *bulgur* is softened but still springy. Drain and dry with absorbent paper towels.

Place the *bulgur*, half the tomato paste and half the ground lamb in the bowl of a food processor and process until almost smooth. Transfer to a bowl. Process the remaining lamb and tomato paste with the onion and ½ tbsp parsley until that, too, is as smooth as possible. Transfer to the bowl. Sprinkle with the spices, salt and pepper to taste, and lemon rind. Work the mixture with your hands until everything is well combined.

Dip your hands in cold water and use to form the mixture into long, thin sausage shapes. Spear each "sausage" with a skewer, and press the meat around it.

Brush the kebabs with oil and cook about 4 in from the coals or grill. Turn the skewers occasionally, and cook for about 10–12 minutes. Arrange the kebabs on a serving dish, top with the pepper and scatter with the reserved parsley leaves.

ARMENIAN SEMOLINA PUDDING

ARMYANSKY MANNY PUDDING

◆ ◆ ◆

**This semolina pudding displays the extravagant
Caucasian sweet tooth which is shared with the Turkish
and Levantine cultures.**

SERVES 4

- ◆ *1½ cups medium white
  wine*
- ◆ *2¼ cups water*
- ◆ *grated rind of ½ lemon*
- ◆ *2½ cups sugar*
- ◆ *juice and grated rind of
  1 orange*

- ◆ *salt*
- ◆ ½ *cup semolina*
- ◆ *2 egg yolks*
- ◆ *3 egg whites*
- ◆ *1 tsp lemon juice*
- ◆ ¼ *cup shelled pistachio
  nuts*

Place the wine, 1¼ cups water, and the lemon and orange rind in an enamelled or stainless steel saucepan. Add a pinch of salt and stir over high heat. Bring to the boil and add the semolina to the pan, stirring. Reduce the heat, and simmer for about 6 minutes until the mixture is thick and smooth.

Stir ½ cup sugar and the orange juice into the mixture, and continue stirring until it boils again. Take the pan off the heat and whisk in the egg yolks.

Whisk the egg whites in a bowl until stiff but not dry. Carefully fold into the semolina, little by little, until all the whites are incorporated.

Preheat the oven to 325°F. Pour the pudding into a fluted mold, and place the mold in a pan. Add enough water to come halfway up the sides of the mold. Bake the pudding for 55 minutes, or until set. Remove from the oven and allow to cool slightly.

Meanwhile, make the syrup. Combine 1 tsp lemon juice with the remaining water and sugar. Bring to the boil, stirring, until the sugar is dissolved. Continue to cook over lower heat until the liquid has become syrupy. Mix in the pistachio nuts.

Turn the pudding over and carefully unmold onto a serving plate. Spoon a pool of syrup and nuts around the foot of the pudding and over the top. Serve the remainder separately in a sauceboat.

ARMENIAN TOASTED BREAD PUDDING WITH SAUCE CREAM

EKMEK KAIMAKSI

◆ ◆ ◆

This is a glorified bread pudding, a nursery dessert as beloved of Armenian expatriate families as it is of those in the old country. The *kaimak* can also be used as a topping for fruit salads, or eaten on its own with a sprinkling of nuts.

SERVES 6

For the kaimak
◆ *3¹/₄ cups heavy cream*   ◆ *1³/₄ cups milk*

For the ekmek
◆ *12-15 x ³/₄ in thick slices Greek, sour dough, or other country-style bread, crusts removed*
◆ *¹/₄ cup milk*   ◆ *2 tbsp water*

For the syrup
◆ *2 cups sugar*   ◆ *1 cup water*

Make the *kaimak* first. In a square or rectangular flameproof casserole or pan with sides at least 2 in high, combine the heavy cream and the milk. Simmer over low heat and scoop out some of the mixture. Lift your arm high over the casserole and let the liquid stream back into the pan.

Continue to scoop and pour the liquid for the next 15 minutes, until the entire surface of the mixture is covered with little bubbles. Lift the pan carefully from the heat, making sure not to agitate it, and move to a warm place. Leave for 2 hours, then move to room temperature for 2 more hours. Then carefully transfer to a refrigerator for 24 hours.

Run a knife around the edges of the pan and cut the top layer of solidified cream into long strips, and then into shorter strips. With a spatula, lift the strips off the milk and transfer to a plate. Cover with plastic wrap and chill. (The *kaimak* will keep for about 5–6 days in the refrigerator.)

To make the *ekmek*, preheat the oven to 325F. Toast the bread slices on a baking tray for 10 minutes, or until they are dried and golden.

Arrange the toasts, in a slightly overlapping layer in a baking dish or shallow casserole. Combine the milk with the water, and pour the liquid evenly over the toast. Set aside.

To make the syrup, combine the sugar with the water in a saucepan. Bring the mixture to the boil over high heat, stirring, then lower the heat slightly until it begins to thicken. Then bring to the boil for 1 minute and remove from the heat.

Set the oven to 350°F. Pour the syrup over the toast, and put the dish in the oven. Bake for 40–45 minutes, or until browned and puffed. Allow to cool to room temperature, then serve with the *kaimak* spooned over the top.

BAKLAVA

◆ ◆ ◆

Armenians are the Viennese of Caucasia – mad about pastries. Perhaps this is because so many Armenians were merchants, and making a sale was traditionally done in a friendly fashion – over tea and cakes. Armenian *baklava*, unlike Turkish versions, are traditionally made in a round pan.

MAKES ABOUT 20

◆ *1 packet phyllo pastry (8 x 12 in)*
◆ *6 cups walnuts, chopped*
◆ *1 tsp cinnamon*
◆ *3¹/₄ cups sugar*
◆ *2 cups unsalted butter, melted*
◆ *1³/₄ cups plus 2 tbsp water*
◆ *2 tbsp fresh lemon juice*
◆ *large pinch of cinnamon*
◆ *2 whole cloves*

Ideally, use a round baking pan 11–12 in in diameter. Unroll the sheets of phyllo pastry, keeping them together, and lay the pan over them. Using a sharp knife or pastry cutter, round off the edges of the long ends. (The width will be too short to trim.) Discard the trimmings and reroll the sheets, covering them with a damp towel to prevent them from becoming brittle.

In a bowl, mix together the walnuts, cinnamon, and ¹/₂ cup sugar. Take out 3 sheets of the phyllo pastry. Butter the pan generously and place one sheet on the bottom. Brush with the butter and cover with another sheet, laid at right angles across the first so that it extends across the width. Brush with butter and cover with a third sheet, at a slightly different angle. Butter that sheet, then sprinkle over some of the nut mixture. Continue layering the phyllo pastry in this fashion until you have used all the nut mixture, then cover the top with 5–6 sheets of buttered phyllo pastry.

Preheat the oven to 325°F. Score the pastry into a diamond pattern, without cutting through all the way. Bake for 50 minutes, or until the top is golden and crisp. Remove from the oven.

Make the syrup by combining the remaining sugar, the water, lemon juice, cinnamon, and cloves in an enamelled or stainless steel saucepan. Follow the method for making the syrup for Armenian Toasted Bread Pudding with Condensed Cream. Pour the hot syrup over the *baklava*, and leave for at least 24 hours so that as much syrup as possible will be absorbed. Cut through the scoring to release the diamond shaped pieces.

DESSERTS

MELON AND WALNUT COMPOTE

KOMPOT IZ DYNI I OREKHOV

◆ ◆ ◆

**Versions of this simple dessert are eaten from
Greece through Georgia and Armenia to Uzbekistan.**

SERVES 6–8

- ◆ *2 small cantaloupe or honeydew melons, halved, seeded, and cubed*
- ◆ *1 1/2 cups honey*
- ◆ *3 cups walnuts, chopped*

Place the melon cubes, with any juice, in a bowl. Add the honey and toss to coat lightly. Stir in the walnuts. Divide the mixture between individual bowls.

6

FROM THE STEPPES OF TARTARY
Central Asia and Kazakhstan

THE ERSTWHILE SOVIET REPUBLICS OF UZBEKISTAN, KIRGIZSTAN, TAJIKISTAN, AND TURKMENIA WERE USUALLY REFERRED TO COLLECTIVELY AS THE CENTRAL ASIAN REPUBLICS UNDER THE OLD ORDER, AND WERE GROUPED TOGETHER WITH KAZAKHSTAN BECAUSE OF THEIR SHARED CULTURE AND HISTORY. FOR THIS IS SILK ROAD TERRITORY: ACROSS THESE DESERTS AND STEPPES CAME THE ARMIES OF ALEXANDER, THE HORSEMEN OF GENGHIS KHAN AND TAMERLANE, AND THE CAMEL CARAVANS THAT BROUGHT MARCO POLO TO CHINA. DESPITE THE CHANGES WROUGHT BY THE ECONOMICALLY DRIVEN SUZERAINITY OF THEIR MASTERS IN MOSCOW, THESE STATES ARE STILL HARSH LANDS, WITH SAVAGE EXTREMES OF TEMPERATURE AND TERRAIN.

Despite the harsh climate and terrain, romance can be found in these regions: in the blue-tiled city of Samarkand and the winding mud-brick alleys of Tashkent, both in Uzbekistan; in the permanently snow-capped peaks of the Tien Shan and Pamir ranges that define the perimeters of Tajikistan and Kirgizstan; in the verdant oases punctuating the sandy wastes of Turkmenia; and in the staggering emptiness of Kazakhstan, 1,180 miles from the Volga to the Chinese border.

This vast area is home to some of the peoples least touched by Sovietization, or indeed by the modern world. The "indigenous" inhabitants are, in reality, a melting pot of races. Mainly Turkic and Persian stock is leavened with Mongolian, Chinese, Siberian, Arab, Gypsy, and tribal strains like the Kazakhs and Kirgiz, varying according to state and local regions. National costumes are everyday wear in many streets; the pervasive Sunni culture means that traditional Muslim generosity and inhibitions are equally observed; old ways of living, trading, and farming are followed in the remotest spots.

Conversely, the influx of non-indigenous people, particularly after the mid-1930s, has meant that Muslims are now outnumbered in all the states. Ethnic Russians, Ukrainians, Armenians, Crimean Greeks and Georgian Turks, as well as groups of other East Europeans, rub shoulders with the natives in the markets and bazaars. Expelled to Central Asia by Stalin's purges and encouraged by Khrushchev's incentives, their parents and grandparents founded stable communities which now flourish in this alien soil. However, riots and violent confrontations have erupted in several regions during the last few years, sometimes between rival groups and sometimes against the dominance of ethnic Russians in positions of authority. Only time will tell if these sporadic outbursts will grow into something more serious.

Though the visitor is still struck by the ageless appearance of many of the cities and villages and by the open space, the programs implemented by the Russian masters have resulted in certain dramatic changes. Camels are fewer, replaced by longhorn cattle. Chemical plants, factories, quarries, and massive irrigation canals disfigure the plains, and in the "Bayconur cosmodrome" in

Kazakhstani Anatoly Tatarenko is presented with a fragrant loaf of bread at the end of the harvest. His team of farm workers achieved the highest level of productivity in the region.

Zhamabek Beisenov, senior shepherd on the Chokan Valikhanov state farm in Kazakhstan, pastures his flock.

Kazakhstan, the empty landscape conceals environmental havoc waged by underground nuclear testing. While the channelling of water resources has resulted in a blossoming of once-arid steppeland, the leaden hand of Communist planning has recreated the 19th-century cotton monoculture of the American South, with 20th-century versions of its economic dependency and soil nutrient erosion. Citrus and soft fruits, grapes, melons, dates, carrots, pumpkins, peppers, and cucumbers flourish in the land allotted to them, but scattered evidence of ecological exploitation and corruption are unhappily obvious even to the unobservant.

Central Asian cuisine is surprisingly homogeneous, in spite of the huge spread covered by the republics, the range of ethnic groups, and the varying productivity of the land. Its prevailingly Mongol and Tartar origins mean that it is spicy and reliant on bread, rice, yogurt and lamb. Recently it has become the most fashionable cuisine in the CIS, with several new restaurants opening in Moscow that specialize in it. This is indeed ironic, since in the local hotels and restaurants that cater to foreigners and better-off citizens, it takes second place to mediocre Russian-style cooking.

Uzbekistan has probably given the most recipes to what is generally termed Central Asian cooking; it is the most sophisticated republic, containing the three best-known centers – Tashkent, Samarkand, and Bukhara. Their central covered markets (*tsentralny rynok*) and farmers' markets (*kolhoznye rynky*) are a riot of color in season, and tourists find their senses assailed with a wealth of new sights and smells. Over 1,000 types of melon are grown in Uzbekistan alone; only an armful are ever seen in the West.

Plov – rice pilaf made with or without chicken or lamb, and enriched with an assortment of fruits and nuts – is a specialty that has variations all over the area. A love of pastries, dumplings, and fritters is another characteristic shared by all the states – *manty, chebureki, gutap,* and *samsa* are filled with lamb, herbs, eggs, onions or mashed pumpkin (*tykva*), depending on the season and area, while *belyashi* is a particular type of deep-fried meat pie found in Kazakhstan. *Non* – the flat onion bread – has a name reminiscent of Indian *nan*, but is in fact more like an Indian *paratha* in looks, taste and texture.

Another border crossing has brought the Georgian and Armenian delight in walnuts to Central Asia. They can be found in soups, in the pastries offered at the teahouse (*chaikhana*) where, in true Muslim fashion, the men meet to pass the time of day – and in *yanchmish*, a sticky candy.

The thick meat soups such as *besh barmak* and *mstava* encountered by the tourist in the very basic hotels and cafés are filling but often unappealingly greasy to Western palates. In fact, grease and fat are a hazard of Central Asian cooking, since the sheep raised there are prized not only for their meat but for the quantity of fat rendered from their rumps and tails. In this they bear a striking resemblance to the sheep of the Levant, another instance of cultural cross-fertilization. *Kazy* (horsemeat sausage), *kurt*, a hard and pungent sun-dried ewe's cheese, and *kumys* (fermented mare's milk), found primarily in Kirgizstan and Kazakhstan, are all tastes to be acquired by the seasoned – and gastronomically adventurous – traveller.

CHILLED VEGETABLE SOUP

HOLODNY SUP-SALAT

◆ ◆ ◆

This is an extraordinarily refreshing soup – like a liquid salad. Based on ingredients found all over the Central Republics, it is a refined variation on a common theme.

SERVES 4–6

- ◆ *3 cloves garlic*
- ◆ *4 thick slices Greek or French bread, crusts removed*
- ◆ *¹/₄ cup butter*
- ◆ *2 red onions, thinly sliced*
- ◆ *8 radishes, thinly sliced*
- ◆ *7 large ripe tomatoes, skinned, seeded, and chopped*
- ◆ *¹/₂ cucumber, peeled and thinly sliced*

- ◆ *salt and freshly ground black pepper*
- ◆ *large dash of Tabasco*
- ◆ *5 tbsp vegetable oil*
- ◆ *1 tbsp lemon juice*
- ◆ *14 fl oz can chicken consommé*
- ◆ *²/₃ cup Greek- or Bulgarian-style yogurt*
- ◆ *8 scallions, finely chopped*

Finely chop two of the garlic cloves and set aside. Use the remaining clove to rub over the bread slices. Roughly cut them into croutons.

Heat the butter in a frying pan and sauté the croutons until golden. Drain and set aside.

In a large bowl, combine the chopped garlic, red onions, radishes, tomatoes, cucumber, seasoning to taste, and the Tabasco. In a small bowl, whisk together the oil and lemon juice, then pour over the salad and chill for 1 hour.

Place the chicken consommé in the refrigerator 30 minutes before you make the soup.

Just before serving, add the chilled consommé to the bowl and stir it in thoroughly, then stir in the yogurt. Sprinkle with the scallions, and serve the croutons in a separate bowl.

YOGHURT SOUP WITH APRICOTS AND WALNUTS

SUP IZ YOGURTA Z ABRICOSAMI I GRYETSKIMI OREKHAMI

◆ ◆ ◆

Some of the combinations and textures of Central Asian dishes seem quite strange to Westerners. Dried fruits are ubiquitous, many of which are unknown here; crunchy tidbits in smooth, cold soups are another surprise.

SERVES 4

- *1³/₄ cup plus 2 tbsp Greek- or Bulgarian- style yogurt*
- *1 cup soda water*
- *6–7 ready-to-eat dried apricots, chopped*
- *¹/₄ cup walnuts, chopped*
- *3 tbsp finely chopped chives*
- *2 tsp finely chopped fresh dill*
- *2 tsp finely chopped fresh tarragon*
- *salt and freshly ground black pepper*

Combine all of the above ingredients in an attractive glass bowl, with seasoning to taste, and stir gently. Chill for 1–2 hours and serve.

RHUBARB TEA

CHAI IZ REVENYA

◆ ◆ ◆

In Uzbekistan and Kazakhstan, rhubarb gleams redly in summer markets. It is eaten raw there, its sour flavor much liked. This sweetened "tea" is more appealing – and very cooling in the sweltering Asian heat.

MAKES 10–12 CUPS

- *4 lb or more fresh rhubarb*
- *1 lemon, thinly sliced*
- *sugar*
- *mint leaves*

Wash and drain the rhubarb. Trim off the leaves and tough bottoms of the stalks. Chop the remainder into small pieces. Use a large cup to measure the rhubarb into a large enamelled or stainless steel casserole, counting the number of cups used. Follow with an equal amount of water.

Bring the mixture to the boil over medium–high heat, stirring occasionally. Reduce the heat and cover. Cook, stirring occasionally, until the rhubarb is pulpy.

Strain the cooking liquid into a wide-mouthed pitcher. While hot, stir in sugar to taste – the less sugar the more thirst-quenching it will be. Leave to cool, then chill. Add slices of lemon and a small bunch of mint leaves. Pour into glasses garnished with more mint leaves.

Until the Russian Revolution, the Uzbek city of Samarkand was a center of Muslim culture, a key staging-post on the Silk Road and, in the 14th century, capital of Mongol ruler Tamerlane's empire.

KAZAKHSTAN LAMB POTATO CAKES
KARTOPHELNYE PIROSHKI Z BARANINOY PO-KAZAKHSKY

◆ ◆ ◆

There are echoes of Afghan and Pakistani cooking in these spicy potato cakes, which resemble *pakhoras*. They would be served with *kumys* (mare's milk yogurt, though today made commercially with cow's milk) in their native land.

MAKES 12

- ◆ *3 medium-sized red potatoes, peeled*
- ◆ *1 onion*
- ◆ *5 large eggs*
- ◆ *³/₄ lb lean ground lamb*
- ◆ *3 tbsp plain flour*
- ◆ *1 tbsp finely chopped flat-leaved parsley*
- ◆ *1 tbsp finely chopped coriander (cilantro)*
- ◆ *¹/₄ tsp ground cumin*
- ◆ *salt and freshly ground black pepper*
- ◆ *2 tbsp clarified butter*

Grate the potatoes onto a tea towel placed on a work surface. Twist the towel to squeeze out as much liquid as possible from the potatoes. Complete squeezing with your hands, then put the potatoes into a large bowl. Grate the onion into the bowl, and beat in the eggs, one at a time. Stir in the lamb, flour, parsley, coriander, cumin, and seasoning to taste.

Melt the butter in a large frying pan over medium-high heat. Add the lamb and potato mixture in amounts of 3–4 tbsp, spreading the cakes with the back of a spatula.

Cook until golden-brown, about 6 minutes a side. Drain on paper towels, and keep warm until all the cakes have been cooked.

DEEP-FRIED KALE AND EGG ENVELOPES
GUTAP

◆ ◆ ◆

The dividing line between *samsa*, *gutap*, and *beliashi* is a slim one, since they are all pastry cases containing many of the same fillings. *Samsas* can be either baked or deep-fried, while *beliashi* are shallow-fried and *gutap* are deep-fried. Here the fresh herbs usual to the latter are enveloped in a melting custard.

MAKES ABOUT 32

- ◆ *8 large eggs*
- ◆ *salt and freshly ground black pepper*
- ◆ *3 tbsp unsalted butter, melted*
- ◆ *1 tsp plain flour*
- ◆ *good handful fresh parsley, finely chopped*
- ◆ *handful fresh dill, finely chopped*
- ◆ *3 tbsp fresh coriander, (cilantro) finely chopped*
- ◆ *4 oz kale, finely chopped*
- ◆ *4 oz scallions, finely chopped*
- ◆ *vegetable oil*

For the dough

- ◆ *1¹/₂ cups plain flour*
- ◆ *²/₃ - ³/₄ cup lukewarm water*
- ◆ *salt*
- ◆ *2 tbsp unsalted butter, softened*

Beat the eggs in a large bowl and season to taste. Beat in the melted butter and the flour. Stir in the herbs, kale, and scallions.

Preheat the oven to 350°F. Butter a baking dish or pan generously, and pour in the egg mixture. Bake in the oven for about 18 minutes, until the custard is just set. Remove from the oven, and leave to cool to room temperature.

To make the dough, sift the flour into a bowl and make a well in the center. Pour in the water, a good pinch of salt and half the butter and, using a plastic spoon or spatula, slowly stir the flour into the wet ingredients until well mixed. Then beat until it becomes a firm dough.

Transfer the dough to a floured surface and divide in half. Cover one half and set aside. Roll the other half into a rectangle, as thin as possible, and fold over once, then over again, until it is four layers thick. Roll out again as thinly as possible, and trim to about 9 x 8 in. Cut the dough into 4 strips lengthways, then divide each strip into 4 equal squares.

Spoon a heaped tablespoon custard onto each square, and draw up the corners to form a packet. Moisten your fingers and pinch the top to seal. Repeat with the remaining 15 or so squares. Cover with a damp cloth and set aside. Roll out the remaining pastry and repeat the process.

Fill a large saucepan or deep-fryer about 4–5 in deep with oil. Heat until it is very hot (but not smoking) and spits when water is dropped into it (about 375°F). Fry the *gutap* in 3 batches for about 3–4 minutes each, turning, until they are golden and crisp. Drain on paper towels. Serve warm.

Kazakhstan Lamb Potato Cakes

STEAMED LAMB DUMPLINGS
MANTY

◆ ◆ ◆

These are a specialty of Uzbekistan, and bear a resemblance to Mongolian pot-stickers and similar Chinese dumplings. The filling is often just ground lamb, but this version is tastier. *Manty* should be eaten with the fingers.

MAKES ABOUT 24

- ◆ *1¹/₂ lb ground lean lamb*
- ◆ *2 small onions, finely chopped*
- ◆ *3 tbsp lemon juice*
- ◆ *¹/₃ cup raisins*
- ◆ *3 tbsp finely chopped mint*
- ◆ *¹/₄ tsp ground cinnamon*
- ◆ *large pinch of cayenne pepper*
- ◆ *salt and freshly ground black pepper*
- ◆ *4 cups plain flour*
- ◆ *1³/₄ cups plus 2 tbsp water*
- ◆ *butter*
- ◆ *1 cup Greek- or Bulgarian-style*
- ◆ *yogurt or ¹/₂ cup white wine vinegar (optional)*

In a large bowl, combine all of the ingredients except for the flour, water, butter, and yogurt or vinegar. Transfer half the mixture to the bowl of a food processor fitted with a metal blade. Process until of a pasty consistency. Set aside and process the remaining mixture. Combine the two meat mixtures.

Sift the flour into a large bowl. Make a well in the center and pour in the water. Turn in the flour and mix thoroughly to make a smooth dough. Halve the dough, leave one half covered in the bowl, and transfer the rest to a floured surface. Roll out thinly into a large rectangle.

Using a cookie cutter or a wide-mouthed jar, cut out 4¹/₂ in rounds. Place a scant 2 tbsp filling in the center of each dough round. Top each with a dot of butter, and pull up the sides of the dough over the filling to make a small purse. Moisten your fingers with water, then twist and pinch the top of each purse to close tightly. Set aside the prepared *manty*, covered with a damp cloth, and repeat the process with the remaining dough and filling.

Add water to a depth of 1–2 in to a large saucepan and bring it to the boil. Place a steamer or colander over the boiling water, add half the *manty*, cover, and lower the heat so the water just simmers. Steam the *manty* for 15 minutes. Repeat with the remaining *manty*. Serve each batch as soon as it is cooked, together with a bowl of yogurt or a small ramekin of vinegar for dipping, if desired.

STEAK TARTARE

MYASO PO-TATARSKY

◆ ◆ ◆

According to legend, Steak Tartare – the most renowned dish to come out Kazakhstan – was discovered by the fabled horsemen-warriors of Tartary. Always on the warpath, and with little or no time to cook their food, they tenderized meat under their saddles to make it palatable raw. In expensive Russian and East European restaurants, Steak Tartare is always a first course; in the West it is usually served as the entrée.

SERVES 4

- ◆ 2 large egg yolks
- ◆ 3 scallions, finely chopped
- ◆ 2 tsp Dijon-style mustard
- ◆ 1 tbsp vegetable oil
- ◆ 2 tsp pepper vodka
- ◆ 1 tbsp bottled horseradish sauce
- ◆ 1 lb fillet of beef, very finely ground
- ◆ 1 tbsp finely chopped capers
- ◆ 1 tbsp Worcestershire sauce
- ◆ salt and freshly ground black pepper

To garnish

- ◆ watercress sprigs
- ◆ radishes, trimmed and scrubbed
- ◆ scallions, trimmed

Beat the eggs in a large bowl. One after the other, stir in the onions, mustard, Worcestershire sauce, horseradish, oil, vodka, and capers. With your hands, gently work the beef into the mixture, and season to taste. Form into 4 patties and arrange on a serving dish. Garnish attractively with the watercress, radishes, and scallions.

BAKED SPICY DUMPLINGS

SAMSA

◆ ◆ ◆

These baked *samsa* bear a distinct resemblance to the more northerly *pierogi*, though the spicing is unmistakeably Asian. They make delicious hors d'oeuvres for a cocktail party – as do all Central Asian pastries, dumplings, and fritters.

MAKES ABOUT 40

- ◆ *1 lb lean ground beef*
- ◆ *2 small onions, chopped*
- ◆ *salt and freshly ground black pepper*
- ◆ *pinch of cayenne pepper*
- ◆ *small handful fresh parsley, chopped*

- ◆ *small handful fresh coriander (cilantro), chopped*
- ◆ *¹/₄ cup toasted pine nuts*

For the dough

- ◆ *1 cup unsalted butter, softened*
- ◆ *1 cup Greek- or Bulgarian-style yogurt*

- ◆ *2¹/₂ - 2³/₄ cups plain flour*
- ◆ *1 heaped tsp salt*
- ◆ *1 egg*
- ◆ *1 tbsp water*

Make the dough first. Cream the butter with the yogurt in a large bowl. Slowly sift in the flour, a little at a time, beating it in after each addition. Add the salt at the same time. Continue until you have used up all but 1–2 tbsp of the flour. If the dough is still tacky, add as much of the remaining flour as is necessary to make it firm. Cover with plastic wrap, and chill for 3–5 hours.

Meanwhile, make the filling. Place the meat, onions, seasoning to taste, cayenne pepper, parsley and coriander in the bowl of a food processor fitted with a metal blade. Process until it is of a pasty consistency. Remove to a bowl and work in the toasted pine nuts. Chill until needed.

On a floured surface, roll out the dough into a large rectangle. With a cookie cutter or lid, cut out 3–3¹/₂ in circles. Spoon a heaped tsp filling on each circle, moisten the edges, and fold the dough over to make a crescent. Use the prongs of a fork to press and crimp the edges of the crescents. Arrange the crescents on an oiled baking sheet, and chill for 30 minutes.

Preheat the oven to 400°F. Make an egg wash by beating the egg with the water, and brush over the crescents. Bake them for about 15 minutes, until golden-brown. Serve warm or at room temperature. (The *samsa* can be frozen. Thaw and reheat in a 180°C/350°F/Gas Mark 4 oven for 15 minutes.)

UZBEKISTAN GRILLED QUAIL OR PARTRIDGE

PYEREPYOL ILI KUROPATKA-GRILL PO-UZBEKSKI

◆ ◆ ◆

Though Uzbekistan is largely desert, it also contains the foothills of the Tian Shan and Alay mountain ranges, in which can be found plentiful game. Grilled quail and partridge are a specialty, first marinated in spices and thick cream

SERVES 4

- ◆ *8 quail or 4 small partridges, cleaned and gutted, heads removed*
- ◆ *6 tbsp fresh lemon juice*
- ◆ *salt and freshly ground black pepper*
- ◆ *2 cloves garlic, crushed and finely chopped*

- ◆ *2 tsp peeled and grated fresh root ginger*
- ◆ *¹/₂ tsp allspice*
- ◆ *¹/₂ tsp nutmeg*
- ◆ *²/₃ cup heavy cream*
- ◆ *vegetable oil*

If using partridge, cut them in half. Place the whole quail or halved partridges in a wide bowl, and sprinkle with the lemon juice and a heaped tsp salt. Toss and rub the birds with your hands, and leave them to marinate for 1 hour. Then add the remaining ingredients except for the oil, toss, and chill the mixture for 3–4 hours, moving the pieces around once or twice.

Prepare the coals of a barbecue or preheat a grill. On each of four metal skewers, either thread 2 quail or 2 halves of partridge. Truss the birds on, if necessary. Brush the birds with oil, and lay them about 4 in above the hot coals or under the grill. Cook for about 20–25 minutes, turning once or twice, until the birds are just cooked through and nicely browned. Serve immediately.

Uzbekistan Grilled Quail or Partridge

POULTRY & MEAT

LEMON-GRILLED LIVER

PYECHEN-GRILL Z LYEMONOM

◆ ◆ ◆

On street corners all over Central Asia, *shashlyk* can be found grilling on portable barbecues, giving off their heady aroma. The most common are variations of lamb kebabs, but liver and chicken versions are also available. Local Muslims would use mutton or lamb fat to moisten their liver but here bacon fat is more accessible.

SERVES 6

◆ *3 lb calves' or lambs' liver, cut into 2 in cubes*
◆ *3 medium onions*
◆ *12 slices bacon*
◆ *¹/₃ cup butter, melted*

◆ *4 tbsp lemon juice*
◆ *salt and freshly ground black pepper*
◆ *lemon quarters, to garnish*

Trim the liver, and remove any membrane. Poach the onions in boiling salted water for 5 minutes. Drain and halve each onion; cut each half into 3 wedges. Stretch the bacon over the back of a knife, and cut each slice in half. Wrap each piece of liver in bacon.

Thread the bacon-wrapped liver onto 6 long skewers, alternating with 3 onion wedges on each skewer. In a bowl, whisk together the butter and lemon juice.

Prepare the coals of a barbecue or preheat a grill. Brush the liver kebabs with some of the lemon butter, season to taste, and cook 3–4 in from the heat, basting occasionally and turning twice. Serve when the liver is browned and crisped on the outside but still pink in the middle, about 10 minutes. Garnish with the lemon quarters.

TURKMENIAN STUFFED PEPPERS

FARSHIROVANNYE PERTSY PO-TURKMENSKY

◆ ◆ ◆

This is a Westernized version of the stuffed peppers one would encounter in Turkmenia. Some of the dried fruits that give it distinction are not found here, but this recipe is still redolent of the Silk Road and the East.

SERVES 6

◆ *6 medium, well-shaped, red sweet peppers*
◆ *1 tbsp vegetable oil*
◆ *1¹/₂ lb ground lean lamb*
◆ *2 small onions, chopped*
◆ *1 cup cooked long-grain white rice*
◆ *3 tbsp sultanas*
◆ *3 tbsp tomato paste*
◆ *2 tbsp honey*

◆ *2 eggs, beaten*
◆ *1 tsp ground allspice*
◆ *¹/₂ tsp ground cumin*
◆ *¹/₂ tsp ground cinnamon*
◆ *large pinch of cayenne pepper*
◆ *salt and freshly ground black pepper*
◆ *1 cup Greek- or Bulgarian-style yogurt*

Cut the tops from the peppers and carefully remove the ribs and seeds from the insides. Rinse and drain the shells.

Heat the oil in a large frying pan and add the lamb. Cook over medium heat, breaking up the lamb with a wooden spoon, until the meat is browned. Stir in the onions, and cook until they are soft and lightly colored. Remove the pan from the heat, and drain off the fat.

Stir in the rice and sultanas; cook for 2 minutes. Add the tomato paste, honey, eggs and spices; season to taste, and combine well.

Preheat the oven to 375°F. Divide the filling equally between the 6 peppers, pressing it down tightly, and pack them into a shallow casserole. Bake for about 40 minutes, until the tops of the peppers are browned and the peppers are soft. Serve hot or cold, with a bowl of yogurt to spoon over the top.

Lemon-grilled Liver

ALMA-ATA PILAF

ALMA-ATA PLOV

◆ ◆ ◆

There are numerous *plov* recipes originating in Central Asia; this one from the capital of Kazakhstan utilizes the rich bounty of fruit which grow there – the apples are particularly famous.

SERVES 6

- ◆ scant $^1/_2$ cup blanched slivered almonds
- ◆ 4 tbsp vegetable oil
- ◆ 1 lb lamb steaks, cubed
- ◆ 2 large carrots, cut into julienne strips
- ◆ 2 large onions, thinly sliced
- ◆ 9–10 dried apricots, chopped
- ◆ $^1/_3$ cup raisins

- ◆ 3 cups long-grained white rice
- ◆ salt and freshly ground black pepper
- ◆ $1^3/_4$ cup chicken stock
- ◆ $^2/_3$ cup orange juice
- ◆ 1 tsp grated orange rind
- ◆ $2^1/_2$ cups water
- ◆ 1 medium red apple, cored and chopped

Preheat the oven to 400°F. Scatter the almonds on a baking sheet and toast in the oven until golden, about 5 minutes. Set aside and turn the oven down to 350°F.

Heat the oil in a large frying pan over medium-high heat. When just smoking, add the lamb cubes and sauté for 6 minutes, or until well browned. Transfer the meat with a slotted spoon to a large casserole.

Turn the heat down slightly and sauté the carrots in the oil for 3 minutes, stirring, then add the onions and continue to sauté for another 6 minutes, until the onions are soft and lightly colored. Stir in the dried apricots, raisins, and rice. Cook for 2 minutes until the rice is coated with the oil and is becoming opaque.

Add the rice mixture to the casserole with the meat. Season to taste, then pour over the chicken stock, orange juice and rind, and water. Bring to the boil, then cover the casserole and transfer it to the oven. Bake for 40 minutes, or until all the liquid is absorbed.

Remove the *plov* from the oven, stir in the chopped apple, and transfer it to a large serving dish, making a neat mound. Scatter the toasted almonds over the top and serve.

UZBEKISTAN SWEET WALNUT BRITTLE

SLADKOYE PYECHENYE IZ GRYETSKIKH OREKHOV PO UZBEKSKY

◆ ◆ ◆

The Central Asians are famous for their sweet tooth – and for their love of nuts. In this dish the two make a perfect marriage, bound by the sweetened evaporated milk common in their desserts.

MAKES ABOUT 1 ½ LB

- ◆ *1 cup light brown sugar*
- ◆ *¹/₂ tsp ground cinnamon*
- ◆ *¹/₄ tsp ground allspice*
- ◆ *¹/₄ tsp ground ginger*
- ◆ *¹/₃ cup plus 1 tbsp evaporated milk*
- ◆ *3 cups walnuts*
- ◆ *¹/₂ tsp vanilla essence*

Place the sugar, cinnamon, allspice, ginger and evaporated milk in a heavy saucepan and stir over high heat for about 5 minutes, or until the sugar dissolves and the mixture reaches soft ball stage (238°F on a sugar thermometer.)

Remove the pan from the heat and stir in the nuts and vanilla essence. Make sure all the nuts are coated, then pour out onto a sheet of waxed paper. Allow to cool, then break into chunks. Store in an airtight container.

WATERMELON ICE

ARBUZNY LYOD

◆ ◆ ◆

The summer months are extremely hot in the arid wastes and teaming towns of Central Asia and Kazakhstan. Vendors sell ices and soft drinks, and while a Western tourist might not risk this watermelon ice on the dusty streets of Tashkent, homemade it is wonderful.

SERVES 4

- ◆ *6 lb watermelon, rind removed, seeded and cubed*
- ◆ *¹/₃ cup plus 1 tbsp sugar*
- ◆ *³/₄ cup water*
- ◆ *4 tbsp lime juice*
- ◆ *1 tbsp grated lime rind*
- ◆ *1 tbsp very finely chopped mint*
- ◆ *fresh mint leaves*

In a blender or a food processor fitted with a metal blade, process the watermelon pulp until it is a smooth, watery purée. Transfer to a bowl.

In a small saucepan, combine the sugar, water and lime juice and lime rind. Bring to the boil, stirring to dissolve the sugar. Reduce the heat and simmer for 6 minutes, then remove from the heat and stir in the mint. Allow to steep for 2 minutes.

Stir the syrup into the watermelon purée and combine well. Pour the mixture into a plastic or freezing container. Freeze until just firm, then decant into the processor bowl and purée again. Return to the container and freeze until firm. Before serving, allow to stand at room temperature for a few minutes.

SAMARKAND-STYLE PERSIMMON DESSERT

KHURMA PO-SAMARKANDSKI

Sharon fruit, a member of the persimmon family, is named for a region in Israel, but varieties of the fruit itself are found throughout the Middle East and Asia. In Central Asia, they would not include the alcohol – but it does give an extra fillip!

SERVES 6

- ◆ *³/₄ cup plus 3 tbsp mandarin, tangerine or blood orange juice*
- ◆ *¹/₂ tsp grated orange rind*
- ◆ *2 tsp cornstarch*
- ◆ *1 tbsp lemon juice*
- ◆ *2 tbsp Sabra (Israeli liqueur) or other orange liqueur*
- ◆ *6 ripe Sharon fruit or thin-skinned persimmons*
- ◆ *4 tbsp pomegranate seeds*

Place the fruit juice, rind and cornstarch in an enamelled or stainless steel saucepan. Bring to the boil, stirring, then continue to stir over high heat until the juice thickens. Remove from the heat and stir in the lemon juice and orange liqueur. Set aside until just warm.

Meanwhile, plunge the fruit in boiling water for 10–15 seconds. Allow to cool, then peel, using a sharp knife. Carefully cut the flesh of each Sharon fruit or persimmon into 8 wedges, and arrange in a fan shape on 6 dessert plates. Pour the warm sauce over half of each fruit fan and into a pool in the center of the plate. Scatter the pomegranate seeds over the top and serve.

DRIED FRUIT AND NUT TART

TORT IZ SUSHYONYKH FRUKTOV I OREKHOV

◆ ◆ ◆

This pastry is inspired by the extraordinary wealth of dried fruits found in the markets of Caucasia and Central Asia. It is chewy, crunchy, melting – and utterly scrumptious.

SERVES 10–12

- ◆ *³/₄ cup sweet white dessert wine*
- ◆ *³/₄ cup honey*
- ◆ *18–20 ready-to-eat dried apricots or peaches*
- ◆ *¹/₂ tsp grated orange rind*
- ◆ *1 cup blanched whole almonds*
- ◆ *3 eggs*
- ◆ *1 tsp vanilla essence*
- ◆ *2 tbsp unsalted butter*
- ◆ *1 cup walnuts*
- ◆ *1 cup cream*
- ◆ *¹/₄ tsp cinnamon*
- ◆ *pinch of sugar*

For the pastry

- ◆ *1 ¹/₄ cup plain flour*
- ◆ *¹/₄ cup sugar*
- ◆ *¹/₂ cup unsalted butter, cut into small pieces*
- ◆ *pinch of salt*
- ◆ *1 large egg yolk*

Make the pastry first. Place the flour, sugar, butter, and salt in the bowl of a food processor fitted with a metal blade, and process until the mixture has the texture of breadcrumbs. Drop the egg yolk through the tube, and continue to process until the pastry forms a ball. Remove and chill for 30 minutes.

Combine half the wine and 2 tbsp honey with the dried fruit and orange rind in an enamelled or stainless steel saucepan. Cook over low heat, uncovered, for 20–25 minutes, until the liquid is absorbed and the fruit is puffed and soft.

Meanwhile, preheat the oven to 350°F. Place the blanched almonds on a baking tray and toast for about 10 minutes, or until the nuts are golden. Remove from the oven. Keep the oven at 350°F.

In a bowl, beat together the eggs, the remaining wine and honey, the vanilla essence and the butter. Beat in the almonds and walnuts. Flatten the pastry with the palm of your hand.

Place in a 10 in springform tin, and press it over the bottom and sides of the tin, pressing it as thinly as possible. Scatter the apricots or peaches over the bottom of the pastry. Pour the egg and nut mixture over the top, smoothing evenly. Bake the tart on the middle rack of the oven for 45 minutes, or until golden-brown. Cool in the tin on a wire rack; remove the rim before serving with cream whipped with the cinnamon and sugar.

Dried Fruit and Nut Tart